ILLUSTRATED GUIDE TO

PLANTS FOR SMALL GARDENS

OLIVER DAWSON

Illustrated by Henry Barnett

TREASURE PRESS

FOREWORD

This book has been written and illustrated to meet the needs of the countless home owners with gardens of modest size. Fortunately, though, in gardening, space – or the lack of it – bears little relationship to the amount of enjoyment gained. Indeed as most of us know, there are many small gardens which are havens of beauty and interest for many months of the year.

Where garden space is restricted, planting material must be chosen with special care. Overcrowding must be avoided at all costs. Similarly, the features included must be on a scale appropriate to the garden overall. Guidance is given on these problems as well as many other aspects of garden making and improvements, including the choice of plants and their subsequent cultivation. O.D.

For their courtesy and assistance, the artist wishes to thank the staff of the Royal Horticultural Society's garden at Wisley and the Syon Park garden centre.

First published in Great Britain in 1971 by
The Hamlyn Publishing Group Limited

This edition published in 1989 by
Treasure Press
Michelin House
81 Fulham Road
London SW3 6RB

ISBN 1 85051 454 2

Printed in Singapore
Produced by Mandarin Offset

CONTENTS

INTRODUCTION

Design

In many parts of the world, gardening has become one of the most popular hobbies of a vast number of people. But, as many of us are only too well aware, the ever-rising cost of building land has resulted in houses being built on plots of ever-shrinking dimensions. Nowadays, therefore, many newcomers to gardening are forced to pursue their hobby in gardens little larger than the proverbial pocket-handkerchief.

This need not necessarily be a disadvantage, for a small garden, properly looked after, can be infinitely more attractive than one on a larger scale that has been neglected and badly maintained.

The conception of exactly what constitutes a small garden has undergone a radical change. Present-day definitions would vary from a quarter of an acre down to a tiny town or suburban backyard. This calls for a completely fresh approach to planning and planting a garden. Now, more than ever before, the greatest possible use has to be made of the space

A town garden in a formal style

A cottage garden

available. Bearing in mind, also, that a garden is primarily a place for relaxation and enjoyment, it should be so designed that maintenance is reduced to reasonable proportions.

In this connection, we can learn a lot from the cottage gardens of past years – gardens, alas, that are rapidly vanishing from the rural scene. Although, due to the force of economic circumstances, the emphasis in these gardens was mostly on fruit and vegetables, since the cottager of former days had to be almost self-supporting in this respect, he, or his wife, usually managed to cram into those small plots a host of flowers so lovely that many of them are still cherished favourites in the gardens of the present day.

This is the kind of effect that we ought to aim at in the small, contemporary garden. It is here that design can play an all-important part. To be effective, the design of a garden should be in harmony with the house and its surroundings. So, although the general principles of the cottage-type garden would be suitable in many instances, they would need modification to be in harmony with the more austere design of

A typical small garden treated in a formal manner

many present-day houses.

Here, formality should be the keynote, with straight paths and rectangular beds and borders. Where single-storey buildings are concerned, the planting will have to be scaled down. Tall trees and large shrubs could rob the rooms of light and even have a dwarfing effect on the building itself when they reach maturity.

Design, too, must take into account the purposes for which a garden is required. Where there are small children or pets, it may be impossible to grow the choicer and more delicate annuals and perennials successfully. In such circumstances, it might be preferable to concentrate on tough and vigorous trees and shrubs, with a lawn containing rye grass that will withstand hard wear.

Where space permits, a delightful effect is obtained if the garden is divided into a series of outdoor 'rooms' by means of interior hedges. A perfect example of this can be seen at Sissinghurst Castle, where each division, although complete in itself, forms part of a harmonic whole.

There is, of course, always the alternative, where a really small garden is in question, of paving the entire area, apart from beds and borders. This is a trend, particularly in North America and Scandinavia, where the climate is not always productive of the velvety and green turf that is the pride of British gardens.

Wherever possible, a garden should be designed so that all of it can not be seen at once. Borders of shrubs or interior hedges with paths that wind round curves and deep bays can bring an illusion of greater space to the smallest of plots.

Paths, beds and borders should be so sited that they offer pleasing vistas, especially from the windows of the main rooms. Herbaceous borders always look better when viewed along their length, and should be sited accordingly.

Choice specimen trees and shrubs of outstanding architectural beauty should also be included as points of interest. A similar focus of interest is provided by sundials, birdbaths, seats and stone figures, but care must be taken not to overdo such ornamentation.

It is always wise to draw up plans on paper before committing oneself to firm design decisions.

The same site as that shown on p. 6 treated in an informal manner

Rake plot level and lay turves in a staggered fashion

BACKGROUND PLANTING

Lawns

No matter how small the garden, some space, wherever possible, should be allocated to a lawn for nothing else provides a better setting for bedding plants, perennials or shrubs.

The best time to lay turf is between October and March. Seed can be sown in spring or early autumn but autumn is the better time since the soil is warmer, germination is quicker and birds are less troublesome.

The thorough preparation of the site for a lawn is essential to success. It should be dug to a depth of about 9 in., raked and then trodden several times to produce a fine crumbly tilth which is firm and level. At the same time, large stones must be removed. Ideally, when a lawn is to be made from seed, it is advantageous to let the site lie fallow for a season before sowing, so that rogue weed seedlings can be eradicated as they appear. This, however, is a counsel of perfection that is not always practicable.

Before laying turf or sowing seed, the site should have an application of a good general fertiliser at the rate of 2 oz. to each sq. yd. This ensures that the seedling grasses get away to a good start but care must be taken when spreading the fertiliser since uneven coverage will result in uneven growth of the grass.

It is also very important to ensure that the grass seed is sown evenly and the most accurate way to do this by hand is to divide the site into square yards with string, decide on the best rate for sowing the seed and divide this into correspondingly accurate portions and sow accordingly. After turf has been laid, cracks and crevices should be filled by brushing a mixture of sand and sifted soil over the surface.

As soon as a lawn is established, regular and careful maintenance is of the greatest importance. Summer applications of fertiliser and selective weedkiller, autumn feeding and spiking in winter to aerate the turf and stimulate root action are all essential operations. Where moss is troublesome, as it often is in badly drained areas, it can be controlled by spiking the lawn to improve drainage. A moss-killing chemical mixture is also available and this can be very effective.

Levelling uneven turf is a simple matter if a square of turf is rolled back as indicated

Replacing worn edges

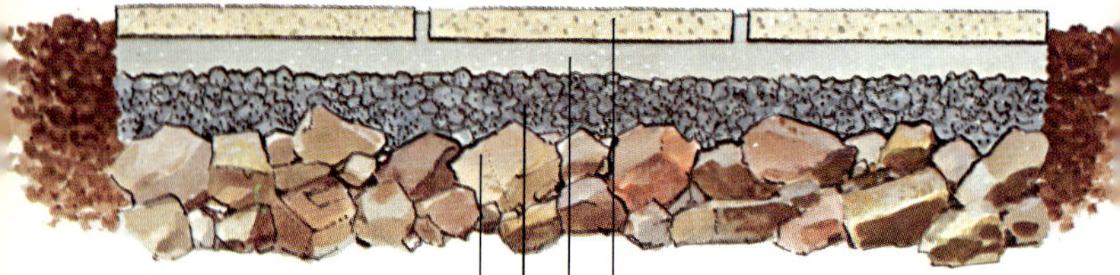

The foundations of a path

Paths

Paths, in addition to providing a means of walking comfortably from one part of the garden to another, can also be a decorative feature in themselves. Wherever possible, the main paths should be at least 2 ft. wide which will allow a person to walk along them with ease.

A path needs a good foundation, not only to provide good drainage but also to guard against wear and tear. A 6-in. layer of coarse rubble, topped up with an inch or two of clinker is ideal for the purpose. In new gardens, it is often possible to collect enough material for path foundations from the rubble left behind by the builders. Large stones, unearthed when digging, are also useful.

There is a choice of surfacing materials for paths to suit every taste. These include gravel, bricks, natural and artificial stone slabs and crazy paving. Natural paving stone gives the most pleasing effect but its price becomes increasingly prohibitive.

Fortunately, there are a number of effective substitutes for natural stone that are a good deal less costly. Concrete paving slabs are obtainable in colours that blend harmoniously into any garden scene. They come in several sizes, including 1- or 2-ft. squares, rectangles of 2 ft. by 1 ft. and even hexagons. By using a mixture of sizes and colours, attractive paving patterns can be made.

A board frame with anchoring pegs keeps the edges straight

Such paving can either be laid dry in a layer of sand or, for a more permanent and hard-wearing path, on a 2-in. layer of concrete. In either case, a dead-level surface is essential. A spirit-level and a large wooden mallet, technically known as a maul, make useful aids to levelling.

Before the slabs are laid, the surface of the concrete should be well tamped down with a board, so that the larger particles of aggregate are below the surface, leaving a layer of wet cement into which it is easy to bed the slabs. Brick paths are laid in a similar manner. It is essential, however, to use the right kind of brick; one, that is, which will not break up in conditions of severe frost.

Fill with cement and work a heavy board to and fro to ensure a level surface. Leave $\frac{1}{2}$-in. spaces between the stones and fill in with cement later

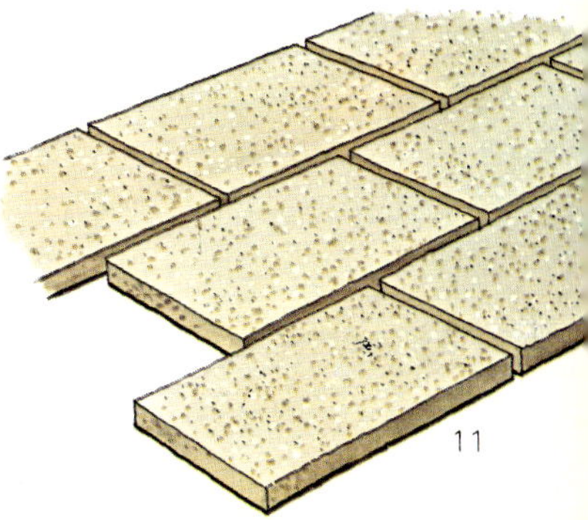

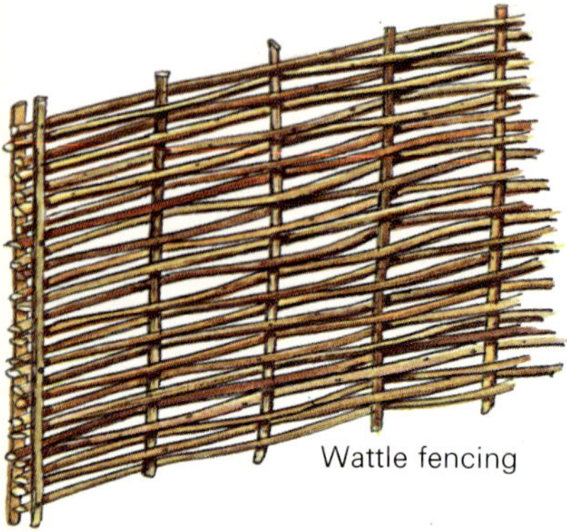
Wattle fencing

Interlap fencing

Concrete screen blocks

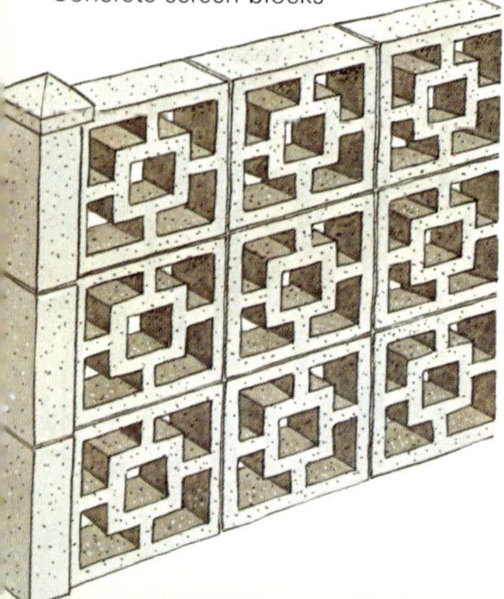

Hedges

One of the first considerations when a new garden is under construction is the provision of shelter and privacy. Screens of wattle or interlapped fencing are an effective temporary stopgap, but they cannot compete with either the beauty or lasting qualities of a living screen.

In the small garden cost need not be such an important consideration as it is where long stretches of hedge are to be planted. In the latter case, expense might dictate the use of one of the less costly hedging subjects, such as quickthorn, privet, beech, hornbeam or lonicera.

The owner of a small garden can afford to be more selective. He can choose from a long list of suitable hedging subjects that includes deciduous, evergreen, coniferous, flowering and berrying shrubs.

Two of the best deciduous hedging subjects do not really rate this description. Although both beech and hornbeam shed their leaves in winter when allowed to develop naturally, they retain their russet autumn foliage throughout the winter when they are grown as hedges and are clipped regularly.

Berberis stenophylla

Beech is the better looking of the two but hornbeam makes a more suitable choice for heavy, moist soils. It can be mixed with quickthorn in the proportion of six of the latter to one of hornbeam. Quickthorn alone makes one of the cheapest hedges obtainable, but in winter its open texture provides little or no privacy.

Less often seen as a garden hedge but very attractive in spring, as well as in autumn, when the small vine-like leaves assume red and orange tints, is the Field Maple, *Acer campestre. Prunus cerasifera nigra* makes a striking hedging plant with leaves of an eye-catching purple. Privet, although a greedy feeder and notorious soil robber, can be used to good effect in town and suburban gardens. It stands up well to town conditions and remains practically evergreen when regularly clipped.

Gardeners who like a more spectacular single-shot display will prefer to plant a flowering hedge, which will look magnificent when its blossom is at the peak. In this category, it would be hard to better two of the evergreen barberries. *Berberis darwinii* has brilliant orange-yellow flowers in April and May, set off to perfection by the polished shield-shaped leaves. *B. stenophylla* flowers a month to six weeks later, with elegant arching sprays of yellow blossom. *Berberis thunbergii atropurpurea*, a deciduous barberry with rich reddish-purple foliage throughout the spring and summer, also makes a most attractive hedge.

Another group of shrubs, of which many members make colourful hedges, are the evergreen escallonias. They are particularly suited to milder areas and seaside districts. Escallonias flower around midsummer and a light pruning immediately the blossoms fade will generally persuade them to stage a repeat performance in autumn. C.F. Ball with deep red tubular flowers is a fine variety for hedging. Equally good are Donard Seedling and *edinensis*, both with pink flowers. The latter is noteworthy for its elegant arching habit of growth.

The Penzance Briars are a group of hybrid shrub roses whose vigorous constitution and amenability to clipping make them particularly suitable for this purpose. All of these, together with the Sweet Briar, *Rosa rubiginosa*, another good hedging rose, have sweetly scented foliage and striking red hips that follow the colourful display of bloom in June. Amy Robsart, Anne of Geierstein and Lady Penzance are varieties

Berberis thunbergii atropurpurea

Sweet Briar hedge

well worth planting as they will make very attractive hedges.

Conifers make dense screens that provide both privacy and garden interest at all seasons. The only drawback is their cost, but the high initial outlay must be set off against subsequent ease of maintenance, since the majority of conifer hedges need only one light trimming annually.

Chamaecyparis lawsoniana fletcheri and *C.l. allumii,* forms of Lawson's Cypress with fine glaucous-blue foliage, make attractive alternatives to the commoner green forms. But perhaps the finest variety of all for hedging is Green Hedger, a fairly recent introduction, that is vigorous and fast growing, with foliage of a brilliant emerald green.

Two other hedging conifers with a rapid growth rate are *Thuja plicata atrovirens* and *Cupressocyparis leylandii.* The latter, which does well in seaside districts and has no objection to chalky soils, is probably the fastest growing conifer in cul-

A hedge of lavender

tivation, making a dense hedge 5 to 6 ft. in height, 3 to 4 years after planting.

Yew, which we seldom think of as a conifer, is one of the most distinguished of all evergreen hedging plants. It has, however, a reputation for slow growth; a reputation that is not entirely deserved. Newly planted yew hedges will put on six inches a year for several years, before slowing down almost to a standstill at maturity.

Evergreen shrubs make good hedging subjects, and these include many members of the berberis and cotoneaster families, and in seaside districts, *Griselinia littoralis*, a shrub especially worth planting for the beauty of its fresh green foliage.

Holly makes a handsome protective barrier, but like yew, it takes a long time to reach a satisfactory height. Laurel (*Prunus laurocerasus*) will grow far more quickly to form a dense evergreen screen. The varieties *caucasica, rotundifolio* and Otto Luyken are all first rate for hedging.

A rhododendron hedge offers the best of both worlds – handsome, evergreen foliage and dazzling beauty of blossom in early summer. *Rhododendron ponticum*, the common species, is the one most widely planted, mainly on account of cost. For those prepared to face the high initial outlay, many of the named hybrids, such as Pink Pearl, make hedges of outstanding beauty.

Ever-grey shrubs are, in the main, fairly compact in character and make useful subjects for interior dividing hedges. Their height will be between 1 to 3 ft. Box edging (*Buxus sempervirens suffruticosa*) is even more compact and is useful as a permanent edging to formal bedding schemes or for defining the borders of the kitchen garden. The species *B. sempervirens* and the variety *B. s. handsworthii* will make taller dividing hedges, up to 6 ft. in height.

Cupressocyparis leylandii

ANNUALS

When the framework and background of the garden picture is completed, it will be time to consider filling in the blank spaces on the canvas with colour. In a new garden, nothing will achieve this more quickly than annuals.

The botanical definition of an annual is a plant that grows from seed, flowers and sets seed all in the same season and then dies. In our gardens, we make wide use of both hardy and half-hardy kinds.

Hardy annuals are those that can be sown out of doors in spring in the positions in which they are to flower. The half-hardy kinds have to be raised under glass and subsequently hardened off in a cold frame before they are ready for planting out. Alternatively, many can be treated in the same way as hardy annuals, provided that outdoor sowing is delayed until all danger of spring frosts is past.

Many half-hardy annuals are among our most valued and widely grown bedding plants. Hardy annuals look

Calendula (*above*) and sweet peas

best in a border devoted to them solely or associated with shrubs and perennials in mixed plantings. In the early days of a garden's life, they make first-rate gap fillers, providing colour and interest while the more long-term plantings are coming to maturity.

Although annuals like a soil that is fairly fertile and friable in texture, very rich soils tend to produce a lush growth of foliage at the expense of bloom. They should not, therefore, be sown or planted in freshly manured ground.

A sunny site suits most of them best. A week or two before sowing, a dressing of bonemeal, at the rate of 2 oz. to the sq. yd. should be lightly forked into the soil surface. The time for sowing will vary from mid-March to the end of April, according to climatic conditions and situations. The surface should be well raked before the seed is sown. To avoid overlapping, it is useful to mark out the various sections with a pointed stick. Seeds should be sown thinly as this prevents overcrowding of the seed-

Love-in-a-mist (*above*) and cosmea

lings when they first emerge.

Some annual seeds are almost microscopically small. These should be mixed with about ten times their bulk of sharp sand or finely sifted dry soil before sowing. The mixture is then sown as if it were seed only, thus ensuring a more even distribution. Nowadays, the seed of some annuals can be obtained in pelleted form. Each pellet contains a single seed which makes the job of sowing and spacing a good deal easier.

Thinning should commence as soon as the seedlings have made their first pair of true leaves and are large enough to handle. At this stage they should be 'singled'. As growth proceeds thinning should continue by stages until the optimum distance for each particular annual is reached. This will vary from around 3 to 4 in. for very small annuals such as alyssum, linaria, nemophila and other similar kinds to a foot or more for taller subjects like clarkias, godetias, larkspurs, mallows, love-lies-bleeding and annual sunflowers.

Sweet peas are better grown separately, trained to

Annual larkspur

Godetia (*left*) and love-lies-bleeding

canes or tall pea-sticks. They can, however, be included in a border of annuals if they are planted in groups at the back and supported by a tripod of tall canes or pea-sticks. Alternatively, one of the newer dwarf strains, such as Knee Hi, which grows only 2 to 3 ft. tall, could be used.

To provide the long-lasting display of bloom for which annuals are so noteworthy, it will be essential to remove spent flowers promptly. If plants are allowed to set seed, flowering will stop.

Many of the tougher hardy annuals can be sown out of doors in August or September to provide early blooms the following year. Among those which respond well to this kind of treatment are calendulas, cornflowers, candytuft, larkspurs, Shirley poppies and Virginian stock.

Slugs can wreak havoc among young annual seedlings and it is advisable to take precautions against them by the use of a proprietary slug bait or pellets.

Half-hardy annuals are better raised when a greenhouse and cold frames are available. A greenhouse will also offer many other advantages, including facilities for propagating many kinds of plants from cuttings, overwintering tender subjects like pelargoniums and providing cut flowers and pot plants out of season for indoor decoration. Boxes of half-hardy bedding plants can be bought very cheaply although, in general, these consist only of the commoner kinds and varieties.

Half-hardy annuals should be sown under glass in March or April. Sufficient heat to maintain a night temperature of about 7°C. (45°F.) will be needed. The seeds are sown in seed-pans, pots or boxes, in John Innes Potting Compost No. 1 or any other suitable proprietary compost.

The containers should be covered with glass and paper until the seeds germinate. As soon as germination has taken place, the coverings should be removed and the containers placed as close to the light as possible.

Watering needs to be carried out with the utmost care. Seedlings must never be allowed to get too dry, but, on the

Scarlet salvia

Zinnias (*left*) and petunias

other hand, over-watering can cause damping off, one of the commonest causes of seedling mortality. A watering-can, with a very fine rose and a long spout, is best for the operation.

As soon as they are large enough to handle, the seedlings should be pricked out into boxes, about 2 in. apart. After growing on, the young plants should be ready for hardening off in the cold frame by the middle or end of April.

One of the major uses of half-hardy annuals is as summer bedding plants. Petunias, salvias, zinnias, stocks and French and African marigolds all make first-rate bedding subjects. Others, like nicotiana, penstemons, gloriosa daisies and many others are useful for filling in gaps in the herbaceous or mixed border.

The taller kinds can be supported by using short twiggy pea-sticks which are placed in position while the plants are in their early stages. By the time the plants come to flower the sticks will be completely hidden by the foliage.

BIENNIALS

Although we treat them as biennials for all practical purposes, many of the spring bedding plants that we sow one year to flower the next are, in fact, perennials. True biennials, as the name implies, take two years to complete their life cycle. Seeds are sown in the early summer of one year to germinate and produce young plants which overwinter and produce flowers in the second year.

Seed is sown out of doors in the second half of May or in early June in a prepared seedbed, the surface of which has been raked down to a fine tilth before sowing. As soon as they have made their first or second pair of true leaves, the seedlings are transferred to a nursery bed or, where there is insufficient space for this, to an odd corner of the garden where they can be grown on until they are ready for planting out in their flowering positions.

The time for planting out can vary, with different kinds of plant, from autumn to early spring. Wallflowers, foxgloves and Brompton stocks, for example, should always go out in autumn. Sweet Williams and Canterbury bells, which are

Mixed wallflowers

later in coming into flower, can wait until March for planting out.

Wallflowers are one of the most popular of all spring bedding plants. Old favourites like Blood Red, Fire King and Cloth of Gold are still widely grown, but the tendency nowadays is to plant mixtures containing a range of skilfully blended colours. Persian Carpet mixture, for example, has an attractive mixture of pastel shades that includes ivory, cream, apricot, rose pink, terracotta and mauve.

For very small gardens, the dwarf bedding wallflowers make useful space savers, without sacrificing anything where brilliance of display is concerned.

Other bedding plants that are easily raised in a similar manner are the double daisies, forget-me-nots, pansies, violas and polyanthus.

The last named, together with other perennials, such as aquilegias and primulas, are very slow in germinating. The seed sometimes remains dormant for six months or more. It is better, therefore, to sow these in boxes or seedpans. Seedlings can be removed and transplanted as they appear.

Any number of popular herbaceous perennials are equally easy to raise from seed. Many of these are included in the lists that follow.

Hardy annuals

Alyssum

Dwarf edging plant; white, pink and mauve flowers.

Calendula

Showy flowers in shades of orange, yellow and apricot.

Chrysanthemum (annual)

Striking single flowers, often marked with second colour.

Clarkia

Tall spikes of double rosette flowers in many colours.

Clary

Grown for its brilliantly coloured bracts.

Cornflower

Good cut flower; new double strains in blue, pink and white.

Eschscholzia

Easy to grow with wide range of brilliant colours.

Godetia

Tall spikes of double pompon flowers in striking colours.

Love-lies-bleeding

Drooping tassel-like flowers, crimson, white or green.

Love-in-a-mist

Attractive blue flowers surrounded by feathery bracts.

Summer Cypress

Fine foliage plant, turning crimson in autumn.

Ten-week stocks

Sweet Sultan
Sweetly scented outsize cornflower-like blooms.

Half-hardy annuals
Ageratum
Fine edger; clusters of blue flowers all summer.
Aster
Good for bedding in various heights, colours and forms.
French and African marigolds
Colourful edgers and bedders; free and long flowering.
Nemesia
Easy to grow, quick-flowering plants, up to 1 ft.
Nicotiana
Good for mixed border; newer varieties stay open all day.
Petunia
Fine summer bedders with a wide colour range.
Ricinus (Castor Oil Plant)
Handsome bronze, purple or green foliage; fine focal plants.
Salvia
Brilliant scarlet bedding plant in various heights.
Ten-week stocks
Splendid flowers for providing colour in June and July.
Zinnia
Showy bedder or edger, wide variety of colours and forms.

Annual chrysanthemums (*left*) and eschscholzia

Biennials
Canterbury bell
Stately spring flowers; bell and cup-and-saucer varieties.
Double daisy
Double daisy flowers for edging or bedding in spring.
Foxglove
Midsummer border plants; Excelsior hybrids notable.
Honesty
Purple spring flowers; silvery seedpods for arrangements.
Forget-me-not
Blue edger; also associates well with tulips, hyacinths.
Sweet William
Gay coloured flat heads in self colours or auricula eyed.
Wallflower
The most popular spring bedding plant.
Siberian Wallflower
Good orange and yellow bedding plant as follow-on to above.

Perennials
Achillea
There are numerous varieties of this easy attractive border plant.

Canterbury bell (*left*) and Sweet Williar

Aquilegia (Columbine)
Lovely bonneted and spurred flowers in a range of colours.
Aubrieta
Favourite rock plant grown easily from seed sown spring, early summer.
Delphinium
Giant and smaller belladonna kinds from seed sown spring.
Globe thistle
Steel-blue drumstick flower heads, thistle-like foliage.
Lupin
Tree lupins and Russell strain are worth growing from seed.
Oriental poppy
Summer border flowers with large striking black centres.
Primula
All hardy primulas come easily from seed.
Pyrethrum
Valuable plants for early cut flowers.
Sweet rocket
Fragrant white or purple flowers, good shade plant.
Veronica
Freely produced spikes of blue flowers in early summer.

Delphiniums

HERBACEOUS PERENNIALS

A herbaceous perennial is a non-woody plant that lives for more than two years, dying back to ground level each winter and shooting again the following spring although most will increase in size and spread with each consecutive season. There are, however, exceptions to this rule. Some, such as bergenias and acanthus, are evergreen and retain their foliage throughout the winter. Others, like ceratostigma and the Cape Fuchsia, *Phygelius capensis,* are partly shrubby in character and make some fresh growth on the previous season's stems. Many gardeners find that the annual resurgence of growth of these plants in the spring almost as exciting as their subsequent flowering.

One criticism often levelled against the herbaceous border is the amount of work entailed in its upkeep. However, by choosing trouble-free perennials, many of which need little or no staking or tying, as well as those of moderate increase

which will not require transplanting and dividing too frequently, work in the border can be considerably lessened. This demands, of course, a little extra planning.

It is, however, a feature which, to be seen to best advantage, needs plenty of space. To make the fullest impact, a herbaceous border should not be less than 6 ft. in width and at least five or six times that in length and in order to enjoy the beauty of such a feature to the full, it should be viewed along its length.

In the small garden, therefore, it may be preferable to use perennials in association with shrubs or as a front for some other feature, like a rose pergola or fruit wall.

The site should be open and sunny, since the great majority of popular plants are sun lovers. There are as well, however, a number of very attractive perennials that will be quite happy in a partially shaded position. Few will tolerate drip from overhead branches so that a position under trees should be avoided.

Acanthus mollis

There is much to be said for the present-day trend towards 'island' borders. These are irregular in shape, set in an expanse of lawn and are viewable from all sides.

If we avoid planting the obvious sprawlers, like the taller Michaelmas daisies, Oriental poppies, shasta daisies and other perennials that keel over at the slightest breath of a summer breeze, there will still remain a wide choice of plants that need no staking or tying or, at most, a few twiggy pea-sticks pushed in among the plants when growth commences.

Hardest to find are tall plants for the back row of the border but even for this position there are a number of five- and six-footers that are capable of standing up for themselves.

Artemisia lactiflora, which grows 5 ft. tall and produces feathery spikes of creamy blossom, makes an excellent perennial for the back of the border. The flowers have a delicate, meadowsweet fragrance and the other great virtue of this accommodating perennial is its lack of invasive tendencies. Clumps remain compact for many years, without the need for division or replanting.

It is a plant that associates well with the Plume Poppy *Macleaya cordata* (syn. *Bocconia cordata*). Coral Plume is the best variety of the latter, with finely sculptured, grey-green foliage of great architectural value in the border. The coral-pink flower spikes appear in July.

The globe thistle, *Echinops ritro*, with its metallic-blue drumstick flowers makes another easy-to-manage back row plant, growing more than 5 ft. tall and thriving in sun or partial shade. The variety Taplow Blue has flowers of a much more intense blue than those of the species.

All the campanulas make excellent trouble-free border plants, but only one species is tall enough to warrant a position in the rear rank. This is *Campanula lactiflora*, with spikes of nodding blue flowers on 5-ft. stems that stand up to the fiercest of summer gales. There is also a soft lilac-pink variety, Loddon Anna, as well as one with deeper blue flowers, Prichard's Variety. The last named is not quite as tall as the

Bergenia cordifolia (*left*) and *Astilbe* Fanal

other varieties of this species.

When we look for trouble-free plants for the middle of the border, the choice becomes much wider. Goldenmosa, Leraft and Tom Thumb are all useful varieties of the ever-popular golden rod. The first two grow only 2 to 3 ft. tall and both produce feathery sprays of golden flowers reminiscent of those of mimosa. Tom Thumb, as might be expected, is a midget variety only 18 in. tall and it is especially suitable for the front of the border.

All the Amellus group of Michaelmas daisies, of which King George is perhaps the best known, stand up well without the need for staking or tying. The Novi-belgii group, from which most of the popular autumn-flowering kinds are drawn are less

Artemisia lactiflora (*above*) and Red-hot Poker

accommodating. Only a few can be safely grown without staking. Jean, a compact deep blue form and the violet-blue Eventide are both satisfactory and other trouble-free forms include three striking reds – Crimson Brocade, Melbourne Belle and Winston S. Churchill. Dwarf forms such as Lady in Blue, Margaret Rose and Snowsprite make excellent edging plants.

Two acanthus species, *A. mollis* and *A. spinosus*, are noteworthy of their finely sculptured evergreen foliage and majestic spikes of hooded purple and white flowers.

Bergenias are grown primarily for the beauty of their fleshy, rounded leaves with the large flower trusses, pink in most forms, providing a welcome bonus in spring. Evening Glow, with bronzy-red winter foliage, is a most striking form.

The ferny foliage of the astilbes complements the frothy plumes of lovely blossom which appears during July and August. Avalanche (pure white), Fanal (crimson-red), Red Sentinel (brick red) and William Reeves (crimson-scarlet) are all worth growing.

Contrast of leaf textures is important in the border and plants with sword-like foliage make an effective foil to any of those already mentioned. They have the added advantage of needing no kind of support. Irises, day lilies, Red-hot Poker and the handsome New Zealand Flax, with its 6-ft. broadsword leaves and unusual flowers of deep mahogany red, all add greatly to the overall interest of a herbaceous border.

Dwarf Michaelmas daisies

Irises

The Bearded Iris, *Iris germanica,* provides some of the loveliest and most colourful flowers in the spring. Where sufficient space is available irises are worth a border to themselves but several generous clumps will add distinction to any herbaceous display. Although the flowering period of individual plants may not be as long as we could wish for, the display can be extended over some six to eight weeks if early, intermediate and late-flowering varieties are chosen. The season will start with the dwarf April-flowering species, ranging in height from 6 to 10 in. and these make ideal edging plants.

When we come to the mainstream varieties, the choice becomes so wide as to be almost embarrassing. Anyone coming fresh to the beauty of the bearded irises, therefore, would be well advised to plant one of the collections offered by specialist growers. These will solve the problems of selection as well as saving money and providing representatives of the best forms and colours. Some idea of the wide range of colours available to those who take advantage of such bargain offers can be deduced from the following names in the novelty collection of a well-known firm of iris specialists. It includes Golden Planet, Blue Admiral, Powder Pink, Brown Trout, Blue Cameo, My Smoky and Canary Bird.

Bearded irises prefer a sunny situation in a well-drained alkaline soil. Acid soils, therefore, will need a generous dressing of lime before the rhizomes go in. July and August are the best months for planting. Once planted, the rhizomes will not require dividing or transplanting for 5 or 6 years. When the time comes, the worn-out tangle of rhizomes at the centre of the plants should be scrapped. It is the younger outer ones, complete with a 'fan' of leaves, that are used as replacements.

The Siberian Iris, *I. sibirica,* is less flamboyant in flower but makes a good permanent plant for the border since its narrow rush-like foliage remains attractive after the flowers have faded. The colour range is more restricted but there are some good blues, as well as white and cream varieties.

I. unguicularis is especially valuable for the colour it provides throughout the darkest days of winter. The secret of success with this iris is to give it a sun-baked position in really poor soil, since it seems to thrive in starvation conditions.

Iris germanica
Iris sibirica
Iris unguicularis

SHRUBS

Not every garden can provide sufficient room for a shrub border, but even the smallest garden will benefit from the inclusion of as large a selection as possible from this outstandingly valuable race of plants. Shrubs act as long-term investments, declaring regular dividends of colour and interest over many years. Once established, the time spent on upkeep is negligible. With many of the more popular kinds, in fact, it is practically a case of 'plant and forget'. Also, it should be remembered that there is a wide range of shrubs available for providing decoration during every season of the year, in the form of flowers, foliage and berries. Even in the depth of winter there are shrubs to provide welcome colour.

Since shrubs will occupy the same position for a very long period, the initial preparation of the site for a shrub border or of individual planting holes, where they are to be grown as specimens, is an operation that should be carried out with great care. Before digging begins, it is a good idea to test the soil in order to find out its degree of acidity or alkalinity. This can be done easily with one of the soil-testing kits on the mar-

ket. This will determine the kinds of shrubs that will flourish and save wasting time and trouble in trying to grow unsuitable subjects.

None of the lovely lime haters, of course, such as rhododendrons, azaleas, camellias and many of the heather species, will thrive in alkaline soils. Many lime-tolerant shrubs, however, will do as well or even better in mildly acid soils, so lime should not be added except where absolutely essential to the health of individual shrubs.

Whenever possible, the site for a shrub border should be dug over some weeks before the plants are due to go in. This will give the soil time to settle and, if such preparation takes place in the late summer or early autumn, there are opportunities of eradicating weeds as they appear.

In most soils, straightforward digging, one spit deep, should suffice. Badly drained and heavy clay soils, however, may need double-digging, sometimes referred to as bastard-trenching, which ensures that the whole site is dug over to a depth of two spits.

At the same time, as much humus-rich material as is available should be incorporated in the lower spit of soil. Such material includes well-rotted animal manures, peat, leafmould, spent hops or matured garden compost. It pays, too, to fork a dressing of bonemeal, at the rate of 2 oz. to the sq. yd., into the surface soil a few days before planting. This slow-acting organic fertiliser will look after the shrubs' needs while they are making new roots and top growth during their first season.

A similar procedure is adopted when the planting holes for single specimens are being prepared. These must always be large and deep enough to take the roots of the shrub without bunching or overcrowding.

Planting shrubs is really a two-man operation, one holding the shrub in position in the planting hole while the other works soil round and between the roots and firms it as he goes. However, any but the largest kinds can usually be dealt with on a 'one man, one shrub' basis. Small specimens and dwarf shrubs can, in fact, be planted with a trowel in a similar manner to bedding plants.

This small shrub with a good ball of soil round the roots is ready for planting. Fork humus into the subsoil

Consolidate the soil around the roots by treading in and apply a mulch over the moist soil

Newly planted shrubs will seldom need staking although this may be necessary on very exposed sites where there is a likelihood of gale-force winds. In any case, it is advisable to go round at intervals during the first season to check for signs of wind rock – a tell-tale depression at the base of the main stem – and firm back any shrubs so affected.

In poor sandy soils, as well as in heavy clays, it pays to replace some of the soil from the planting hole with finely sifted compost, good fibrous loam or with one of the proprietary planting media. It is important also to be aware of the kind of conditions preferred by the subjects being planted. The majority of shrubs prefer a position in full sun; others opt for partial shade, while a large number seem to be equally happy in either full sun or partial shade. The lists of shrubs by season, given on p. 46–57, includes this information.

Mulching is an operation that is vitally important to the well-being of newly planted shrubs during their first spring and summer. Mulching helps to conserve soil moisture by checking evaporation and the operation

should be carried out when the ground is moist, even if this means watering the soil before applying the mulch.

Partly rotted leaves or compost, peat and chopped bracken all make excellent mulches. Grass clippings, too, can be used in summer, provided that the lawn has not been recently treated with selective weedkillers.

Although the peak period for colour in the shrub border is from May to July, it is possible, by careful selection, to have something in bloom at every season of the year, including the darkest days of winter. Quite a number of shrubs flower between November and the end of February. The winter heaths, in particular, provide a blaze of colour from January to March even in the severest of winters.

What many other winter-flowering shrubs lack in flower power they make up for in fragrance. *Viburnum fragrans*, the Winter Sweet, *Chimonanthus praecox* and *Daphne mezereum* will scent the air for yards around, while the curious spidery blossoms of the Witch Hazel, *Hamamelis mollis*, have a delicate perfume that will scent an entire room if sprigs are cut and brought indoors.

However, the bulk of the shrub planting in any garden should consist of good all-rounders which, in addition to providing a lavish display of blossom have a second string to their bow in the shape of autumn leaf colour, bright berries or

1 *Viburnum tinus*
2 *Spartium junceum*
3 *Acer japonicum aconitifolium*
4 *Buddleia davidii* White Cloud
5 *Syringa vulgaris* Katherine Havemeyer
6 *Erica carnea* Springwood White
7 *Weigela florida variegata*
8 *Forsythia intermedia* Lynwood
9 *Hibiscus syriacus* Woodbridge
10 *Berberis darwinii*
11 *Philadelphus* Enchantment
12 *Cotinus coggygria* Royal Purple
13 *Hydrangea macrophylla* Blue Wave
14 *Potentilla fruticosa* Katherine Dykes
15 *Hebe anomala*
16 *Daphne mezereum*
17 *Phlomis fruticosa*
18 *Phormium tenax*
19 *Exochorda racemosa*
20 *Chimonanthus praecox*

attractive winter bark. Such a double display is of especial importance in the small garden, for obvious reasons.

Winter-flowering shrubs are best sited at vantage points where their beauty can be enjoyed in comfort, either from the house windows, or from the close vicinity of the house itself.

Shrubs with attractive winter bark can provide a valuable contribution to the garden scene in winter. The scarlet-and yellow-barked willows and dogwoods, seen on a sunny winter's day against a backcloth of snow, present an outstandingly lovely garden picture. There are, as well, the curiously marked stems of the Snakebark Maples, the corky winged branches of *Euonymus alatus*, the polished mahogany trunk of *Prunus serrula* and the soot-and-silver trunks of the silver birches all making a decorative contribution to the overall winter picture.

In autumn, most of the colour in the shrub border will be furnished by leaves and berries. The problem of bridging the gap between the brilliant blossom of June and July and the scarlet and gold of the autumn foliage is one that can be solved by including shrubs that flower in August and September, such as *Buddleia davidii*, the butterfly bush, tree hollyhocks, the Blue Spiraea, *Caryopteris clandonensis*, *Perovskia atriplicifolia*, the Afghan Sage with the almost unpronounceable name, and others.

Even in the smallest of town or suburban gardens, a certain number of shrubs can be grown. There are a number of delightful dwarf shrubs, some of which are perfect replicas, in miniature, of their taller relations. These can be used to produce pleasing garden effects on a reduced scale.

The use of shrubs such as these affords the town dweller who enjoys a garden but likes to get away at weekends an opportunity of having one that is always trim and pleasant to look at and yet entails only a minimum of upkeep.

Some of the loveliest of the dwarfs are found among the barberries. They include species and varieties noteworthy for their flowers, berries or foliage. For example, *Berberis stenophylla corallina nana* makes a dense, low-spreading plant not exceeding 2½ to 3 ft. in height. In May, the branches are covered in brilliant orange flowers the beauty of which is set off by the polished evergreen foliage. Slightly taller, with an elegant arching habit, are Crawley Gem and *gracilis*, both of which make first-rate dwarf evergreens where space is restricted.

Berberis thunbergii atropurpurea is one of the most outstanding of the deciduous barberries, equally noteworthy for its summer and autumn leaf colour. This is a characteristic shared by the dwarf form *atropurpurea nana* which grows only 2 ft. tall. The foliage, which is a striking purple during the

1 *Rosmarinus officinalis* Tuscan Blue

2 *Berberis thunbergii atropurpurea nana*

3 *Perovskia atriplicifolia*

4 *Ceratostigma willmottianum*

5 *Lavandula spica* Twickle Purple

6 *Caryopteris* Heavenly Blue

7 *Hypericum patulum henryi*

8 *Viburnum davidii*

9 *Genista hispanica*

10 *Berberis buxifolia nana*

11 *Potentilla fruticosa* Tangerine

12 *Cotoneaster dammeri*

13 *Hebe armstrongii*

summer months, turns an eye-catching fiery crimson with the coming of the colder days of autumn.

Most grey- and silver-leaved shrubs are relatively compact and the attraction of a border of dwarf shrubs will be enhanced if specimens of these, such as lavender, rosemary, santolina, artemisia and senecio, are included in the planting plan.

For those unable to find room for the more exuberant varieties of the butterfly bush, *Buddleia davidii,* there is a delightful pygmy form *B. fallowiana* Lochinch with pale lavender flower spikes, soft, grey-felted foliage and an ultimate height of not more than 4 to 5 ft.

Viburnums are among the most popular of garden shrubs and there is an attractive dwarf species that is grown primarily for the beauty of its fine evergreen foliage. *Viburnum davidii* has oval leaves deeply etched with veins. If both male and female forms are planted, this compact shrub will produce attractive berries in autumn.

Both rock and sun roses are compact and are seen at their best in poor dry soils. This makes them a good choice for the small garden on hot sandy soil. The sun rose, *Helianthemum nummularium,* has a wide range of brilliant colours with heights ranging from 3 in. to 1 ft. Rock roses are taller and their colour range is more restricted but it includes some striking whites, pinks, purples and maroons.

Chimonanthus praecox

(a) SHRUBS FOR WINTER COLOUR

	Botanical Name	Height *in ft.*	Spread *in ft.*
	Chimonanthus praecox	8–10	10–12
	Daphne mezereum	3½–4	3½–4
E P/S	*Erica carnea &* varieties	1–1½	1–2
E S	*Fatsia japonica*	7–10	10–15
E P/S	*Garrya elliptica*	8–12	8–12
	Hamamelis mollis	12–18	12–15
	Kolkwitzia amabilis	6–8	6–9
	Lonicera fragrantissima } *Lonicera* x *purpusii* }	6–8	7–10
E P/S	*Mahonia japonica*	5–7	8–12
P/S	*Viburnum* x *bodnantense*	9–12	10–12
E S	*Viburnum tinus*	7–10	8–10

Code E = Evergreen. P/S Will thrive in partial shade. S Will thrive in full shade.

Garrya elliptica (*left*) and *Hamamelis mollis*

Description	Flowering Season
Waxy yellow scented flowers, centre blotched purple.	Dec–Jan
Purple or white hyacinth-scented flowers, fairly short-lived shrub.	Jan–Mar
Pink, white or purple flower spikes.	Dec–Mar
Large clusters of ivory drumstick flowers, handsome palmate foliage.	Nov
Striking 9-in. jade-green catkins.	Feb
Scented yellow spider-like flowers.	Dec–Feb
Pale brown peeling bark in winter.	Dec–Mar
Creamy-white scented flowers.	Jan–Feb
Magnificent pinnate foliage, long spikes of scented flowers.	Feb–Mar
Upright vase-shaped habit, sprays of pink scented flowers opening throughout winter.	Nov–Feb
White flower clusters, pink in bud, profusely borne.	Jan–Apr

Fatsia japonica

(b) SHRUBS FOR EARLY SPRING

	Botanical Name	Height *in ft.*	Spread *in ft.*
	Amelanchier canadensis	10–15	10–15
		(when grown in bush form)	
E P/S	*Berberis buxifolia nana*	2½–3	4½–6
E P/S	Camellia species & hybrids	various, up to 15 x 15	
P/S	*Chaenomeles speciosa*	Wall shrubs up to 15 ft. spread.	
	Cornus mas variegata	8–10	12–15
	Corylopsis spicata	5–7	6–8
E	*Erica arborea alpina*	7–10	8–12
E	*Euphorbia wulfenii*	3½–4	5–6
P/S	Forsythia species & varieties	various, up to 8 x 8	
P/S	*Kerria japonica fl. pl.*	8–10	8–10
E S	*Mahonia aquifolium*	3–6	3–6
E	*Osmanthus delavayi*	7–10	9–12
P/S	*Ribes sanguineum*	6–10	9–12

Camellia x williamsii Donation (*left*) and *Kerria japonica*

Description	Flowering Season
Foaming mass of white blossom; good autumn leaf colour.	Apr
Amber flowers, deep leaf colour.	Mar–Apr
Magnificent polished foliage; wide colour range of single and double forms.	Mar–Apr
White, pink, red, salmon, terracotta.	Mar–Apr
Masses of small yellow flowers on bare branches; silver-variegated foliage.	Feb–Mar
Hanging clusters of pale yellow, cowslip-scented flowers.	Mar–Apr
Scented white flower spikes; emerald-green feathery foliage.	Mar–Apr
Lime-green bottlebrush flower spikes.	Mar–Apr
Tubular flowers in various shades of yellow.	Feb–Mar
Yellow pompon flowers.	Apr–May
Holly-like foliage; butter-yellow flower trusses followed by purple fruits.	Mar–Apr
Fragrant white tubular flowers; interesting evergreen foliage.	Apr
Pink or crimson flower clusters.	Mar–Apr

Ceanothus (*left*) and weigela

(c) **SHRUBS FOR EARLY SUMMER**

	Botanical Name	**Height** *in ft.*	**Spread** *in ft.*
E	*Berberis stenophylla*	10–12	10–15
	Buddleia alternifolia	12–20	15–20
E	Ceanothus x Delight	15–18	15–20
E P/S	*Choisya ternata*	6–9	8–10
	Cornus florida rubra	12–15	18–20
	Cytisus praecox	6–7	4–6
	Daphne x *burkwoodii*	3–4	5–7
P/S	*Deutzia* x *elegantissima*	4½–5	5–7
E	*Genista hispanica*	2½–4	5–8
P/S	*Spiraea* x *vanhouttei*	8–10	8–10
	Syringa vulgaris hybrids	various	
P/S	*Viburnum tomentosum plicatum*	6–9	7–10
	Weigela	5–7	3–4

Cytisus praecox (*left*) and *Syringa* Mme Lemoine

Description	Flowering Season
Yellow flowers, dark green leaves.	May
Weeping habit, soft purple flowers.	May
Rich blue flowers, dark green leaves.	June
Very fragrant stellate flowers; good wall shrub.	May
Rosy-red bracts, good autumn leaf colour.	May
Compact rounded bush, smothered in creamy-yellow flowers.	May
Medium-sized shrub with mauve, intensely fragrant flowers.	May
Arching sprays of rosy-purple flowers	May–June
Spiny cushion smothered in golden flowers.	May–June
Arching stems of white flowers; good autumn leaf colour.	May
White, pink, mauve, lilac, single and double flowers.	May–June
Tiered branches, white snowball flowers.	May–June
Masses of showy trumpet flowers.	May–June

(d) **SHRUBS FOR HIGH SUMMER**

	Botanical Name	Height *in ft.*	Spread *in ft.*
	Aesculus parviflora	8–12	12–18
	Buddleia davidii varieties	9–12	9–12
P/S	*Clethra alnifolia paniculata*	7–9	8–10
	Genista aethnensis	15–20	15–18
	Hydrangea paniculata	6–8	6–8
P/S	*Hypericum patulum*	3–4	4–5
E	*Lavandula spica*	3–4	3½–4
ES	*Olearia haastii*	6–9	8–12
	Philadelphus		various
E	*Santolina chamaecyparissus nana*	1½–2	2½–3½
E	*Senecio cineraria*	2–2½	3–4
	Spartium junceum	9–12	7–8
	Tamarix pentandra	12–15	15–18

Philadelphus Virginal

Description	Flowering Season
Spikes of white horse chestnut 'candles'	July–Aug
White, red and purple flower spikes, beloved of butterflies.	July–Aug
Long white pointed flower spikes with spicy fragrance.	Aug
Almost leafless stems, golden scented broom flowers	July
White conical flower trusses tinged with carmine-pink as they mature	July–Aug
Masses of golden-yellow chalice flowers	July–Aug
Lavender flower spikes, ever-grey foliage	July–Aug
White daisy flowers; good seaside shrub	July–Aug
Intensely fragrant, creamy-white flowers	June–July
Yellow flowers, silver-frosted foliage	July–Aug
Grown for its finely cut felted silver foliage	July–Aug
Yellow broom flowers on rush-like stems	July–Aug
Feathery foliage, pink scented flowers.	July–Aug

Buddleia davidii (*left*) and *Hydrangea paniculata*

(e) **SHRUBS FOR LATE SUMMER**

	Botanical Name	**Height** *in ft.*	**Spread** *in ft.*
	Abelia grandiflora	6–8	6–8
	Callicarpa giraldiana	5–6	5–7
	Caryopteris x *clandonensis*	3–5	4–6
	Ceratostigma willmottianum	2–3	3–4
	Clerodendrum trichotomum	10–12	12–15
E S	*Fatsia japonica*	7–10	10–15
E	*Helichrysum angustifolium*	2½–3	3–4
	Hibiscus syriacus varieties	8–10	7–10
P/S	*Hydrangea macrophylla* Blue Wave	5–6	7–9
	Perovskia atriplicifolia	6–8	7–9
	Sorbaria aitchisonii	5–8	8–9

Hydrangea macrophylla

Description	Flowering Season
Loose and spreading habit; pink tubular flowers; good wall shrub	Aug–Sept
Pink flowers followed by interesting violet berries	Aug–Sept
Grey-green foliage, rich blue flowers	Sept–Oct
Slaty-blue flowers followed by attractive russet seedheads	Aug–Oct
White scented flowers followed by turquoise berries	Aug–Sept
Handsome palmate leaves, striking creamy drumstick flower heads	Oct
Feathery grey foliage, yellow flowers	Aug–Sept
Grey bark; blue, pink, red and white hollyhock flowers	Aug–Sept
Lacecup flowers in flat heads pink or blue according to soil	Aug
Grey-felted leaves and shoots, blue flowers	Aug–Sept
Large ash-like divided leaves; magnificent plumes of white blossom	Aug–Sept

Caryopteris x *clandonensis* (*left*) and *Hibiscus syriacus* Blue Bird

Spiraea thunbergii

(f) **SHRUBS FOR AUTUMN LEAF COLOUR**

Botanical Name	**Height** *in ft.*	**Spread** *in ft.*
Acer palmatum Osakazuki	15–20	15–20
Berberis thunbergii	6–8	7–9
Enkianthus campanulatus	5–7	4–5
Euonymus alatus	6–8	8–10
Fothergilla monticola	5–8	5–7
Rhus cotinus	12–16	12–15
Spiraea thunbergii	5–7	6–9
Viburnum opulus sterile	10–15	12–15

In addition to the above-mentioned shrubs, there are many whose striking fruits and berries bring welcome colour to the garden in autumn.

Viburnum opulus sterile

Description

Small-leaved maple with brilliant scarlet autumn leaf colour
Apple-green leaves turning dazzling crimson
Clusters of yellow bell flowers edged with red; rich autumn leaf colour
Carmine pink autumn leaf colouring; curious corky winged stems
White mophead flower clusters; brilliant red autumn leaves
Feathery inflorescences give this shrub its popular name; leaves turn guinea gold in autumn
Sprays of dainty white blossom in spring; lacy foliage, pale green turning terracotta autumn hues
Spherical flowers, jade green in bud, turning white as they open; leaves turn a deep wine purple.

Many of these are mentioned in the text.

ALPINE PLANTS

For those who are prepared to face the extra work involved in maintenance, a rock garden can be one of the most rewarding of garden features, especially where the natural contours of the garden lend themselves to its construction without the need for extensive outlay and labour.

Although many alpine plants are in need of special care and protection, there are also any number that will flourish in a variety of soils and situations. These are the ones that the newcomer to this type of gardening should choose for his initial plantings. The more exclusive kinds which need careful cosseting for success can be planted later, when more experience has been gained.

The proper methods of rock garden construction are too wide a subject to be dealt with here, but there are many useful books that deal with this matter in full detail. Although primarily a spring and summer feature, the season of interest can be easily extended by the use of dwarf conifers, small bulbs and later-flowering annuals and perennials.

A dozen or so of the more popular alpine species should find a place in any initial planting. These include aubrieta, arabis,

Iberis sempervirens

Alyssum saxatile (*left*) and aubrieta

Alyssum saxatile and the perennial candytuft, *Iberis sempervirens*. Of the many lovely named forms of aubrieta, Dr Mules, with violet-blue flowers; Mrs Rosewald, bright red; Bressingham Pink, Crimson Queen, and the deepest purple of all, Gurgedyke, are all well worth growing. After flowering, aubrietas should be sheared right back to ground level to prevent the plants from getting too leggy. They will appreciate an occasional dressing of lime in autumn.

There are several good varieties of *Alyssum saxatile,* including *compactum* with golden-yellow flowers, *citrinum,* lemon yellow and Silver Queen with pale yellow flowers and silver-grey foliage. Among the varieties of perennial candytuft worth growing are Little Gem with dark evergreen foliage and *commutatum,* a very free-flowering form.

Rock and cheddar pinks, thrift, moss phlox (*P. subulata*),

that delightful miniature daisy Dresden China, the blue lithospermums, which need lime-free soils and the aizoon and kabschia saxifrages, whose requirements are a gritty soil and good drainage, will all make a first-rate spring display in the beginner's rock garden.

Later in the year the smaller creeping campanulas, such as E.K. Toogood and *C. portenschlagiana,* together with the dwarf *Polygonum vaccinifolium,* sun roses and miniature hypericums will help to provide continuity of colour and interest. Where space permits, clumps of winter-flowering heathers will carry the display right through from November to March.

The uses of alpines need not be confined to the rock garden proper. Many can be employed in other capacities – as plants for dry walls, trough gardens or for filling crevices in paved walks or patios. Some such plants seem positively to like being trodden underfoot; others will be better when planted in parts of the paving where they are less likely to undergo this kind of treatment continuously. In the former category are garden varieties of two popular culinary herbs – mint and thyme. *Mentha requienii,* for example, makes a dense mat of aromatic foliage, spangled, in June and July, with tiny mauve flowers.

Thymus serpyllum

Thrift

Prostrate forms of *Thymus serpyllum,* all with the typical aroma of the kitchen variety, include the white-flowered *albus,* Annie Hall, with flowers of a delicate pink and *coccineus,* an interesting red variety.

Among the less commonly seen carpeting plants are *Antennaria dioica minima,* grey leaved with pink flowers, *Hypericum reptans,* a tiny creeping St John's Wort, *Pratia angulata,* whose white flowers are followed by purple berries and *Raoulia australis,* which lays down a dense carpet of silvery foliage.

Another effective way of using alpines, especially where garden space is restricted, is in a sink or trough garden. This method is very effective for choice or difficult subjects since it is easier to provide the good drainage and the soil conditions that suit these best.

Old stone sinks are ideal but nowadays they are expensive and difficult to come by. The construction of a sink or trough is, however, comparatively easy and there are a number of different materials available including walling stone and cement. For most rock plants grown in this manner a suitable compost would consist of equal parts of loam, leafmould, peat and sand. Adequate drainage is essential.

On a small plot, where space cannot be found for a proper rock garden, there are still opportunities for growing a wide variety of alpines and rock plants, since many will thrive in a dry wall and this can be a very attractive feature.

A dry wall provides one of the most effective ways of treating changes in garden levels. Its construction is a relatively simple matter, well within the capabilities of the average handyman. In the crevices between the courses, as well as on top of the dry wall, many of the easier alpines and other similar plants can find a home. Wherever possible, it is better to get such plants into position while the wall is actually under construction.

Among those especially suited to these conditions are aubrieta, *Alyssum saxatile* and *Iberis sempervirens*. Aubrieta, in fact, is seldom seen to better effect than when its trailing sprays of blossom are allowed to flow down the surface of a wall in a cascade of purple. Thrifts, too, look especially right in this situation.

Flowering at about the same time as the plants mentioned above is a delightful little rock plant with rose-pink flowers rather like those of the annual candytuft. This is *Aethionema* Warley Rose, which looks well in association with the pure white flowers of *Iberis sempervirens*. Further contrasts can be provided by the brilliant colours of the named varieties of the lovely moss phlox, *P. subulata*.

Many of the smaller hardy geraniums can be planted between the courses of a dry wall, including the 6-in. *Geranium dalmaticum,* with blooms of a clear rose pink, and *G. sanguineum* Nyewood, whose flowers are a rich purple.

Later in the year, colour continuity can be provided by dwarf perennials such as rock pinks and campanulas. The evergreen, fleshy rosettes of the sempervivums, or houseleeks, will also be useful in providing winter interest, especially those of the fascinating Cobweb Houseleek, *Sempervivum arachnoideum*.

Where the soil is chalky, the Spur Valerian (*Centranthus ruber*) would make a good choice for naturalising in dry walls. The handsome spikes of crimson, pink or white flowers stand proudly erect against the wall surface and provide welcome colour from midsummer onwards.

1 *Sedum spathulifolium* **2** *Sedum sediforme*
3 *Sempervivum tectorum cantabricum*
4 *Sempervivum arachnoideum* **5** *Valerian*

HEATHERS

A heath garden makes a pleasing and more easily maintained substitute for a rock garden, but where space does not permit its inclusion as a separate feature, groups of heathers can be planted at the foot of the shrub border, or they can be used to provide a colourful and trouble-free edging to a drive.

The most brilliant splash of colour to be found in the garden during the winter months is provided by the winter heaths, varieties of *Erica carnea*. Unlike most other heathers, these are tolerant of lime and they offer a wide range of colour and cover the whole of the winter season. In acid soils, *E. carnea* can be planted in association with summer-flowering heathers to provide continuity of colour and interest throughout the year.

Like all other heather species, *E. carnea* and its varieties need little in the way of attention, once established. When first planted, however, they will appreciate a few handfuls of peat or leafmould in the planting holes.

Planting in groups of three or more of a kind produces a more striking effect than a mixture of single plants of different varieties. Apart from the cutting out of dead flowers in April to keep them compact and counteract any tendency to straggle, the plants will require very little else doing to them.

One of the first of the winter heaths to flower, starting in

King George

November, is King George, a compact, low-growing heather with flowers of a deep purplish-pink. It is closely followed by the inaptly named December Red, since the flowers are closer to pink than to red and it is considered to be a great improvement on the old favourite, Springwood Pink. The latter's white counterpart, Springwood White, still holds pride of place as one of the best varieties for use as ground cover, with a spread of up to 2 ft. at maturity.

Ruby Glow and Vivellii, both of which are in flower in January and February, are worth inclusion for their bronzy winter foliage, which makes such an effective contrast to the carmine pink of their flowers. Varieties of the hybrid *E.* x *darleyensis,* which is also tolerant of lime, will help to supplement the beauty of the foregoing. Other hybrid heathers include Arthur Johnson, with long flower spikes of a brilliant magenta from December to April, and Silberschmeise, which is one of the loveliest of all the winter-flowering heathers.

In June, the Cross-leaved Heath, *Erica tetralix,* together with the Cornish Heath, *E. vagans* and the lovely bell-flowered St Daboec's Heath, *Daboecia cantabrica,* will provide continuity of colour until the Scottish heathers begin their long flowering season in late July or early August.

All varieties of the Cross-leaved Heath have grey-green

Springwood Pink Vivellii

A heather garden in summer

foliage which makes an attractive foil for the flowers. Their flowering season lasts from June to October and the species has large rosy-pink flowers. There are two good white forms, *alba* and *mollis*, while *lawsoniana* is a useful dwarf variety with pink flowers.

Starting to flower in July, the Cornish Heaths have a dwarf spreading habit with long sprays of bloom that remain attractive over a long period. These turn a warm russet brown after they fade and are still decorative when the time comes to clip the plants in February.

Lyonesse is the best white variety, with contrasting golden-brown anthers; Mrs D. F. Maxwell, considered by many to be the finest of all garden heaths, has flowers of a deep cerise pink. Another popular variety, St Keverne is noteworthy for its lovely clear pink flower spikes.

However, the main summer display from August to October, when the wild heathers, too, are ablaze with colour, is provided by the Scottish Heath, *Calluna vulgaris*. As well as

the typical heather colours and some striking double whites, the species includes varieties that are grown primarily for the beauty of their coloured foliage. Such varieties must have a place in full sunlight if this colouring is to develop to its most intense. Of these *searlei aurea,* with bright golden foliage, is the best known. Others equally striking are Gold Haze, whose name is sufficient description, *searlei argentea,* with silvery-white young shoots and *cuprea* whose young golden growths turn coppery orange in winter.

Of the varieties grown for their flowers, it would be hard to better H.E. Beale with extra-long spikes of double pink flowers. J.H. Hamilton is another worthwhile variety considered by many to be one of the best of the smaller heathers, with masses of double flowers, rich pink in colour.

Finally, to bridge the gap before the winter heathers start to show colour again, there is the variety Peter Sparkes whose brilliant double crimson-pink flowers are still in top condition at the end of October.

PLANTS FOR DIFFERING ENVIRONMENTS

Shade

Soil, aspect and climate all play an important part in determining the kinds of plants that can be successfully grown in our gardens. Fortunately, the choice is wide for almost any permutation and combination of conditions. The wise gardener soon comes to realise that it is better to grow plants that are happiest in his particular set of conditions rather than to try and cosset others in an effort to make them flourish in a totally unsuitable environment.

Although the first preference of a large majority of our most popular garden plants is for a sunny, open situation, many of these do not object to partial shade, provided that it is not accompanied by drip from overhanging tree branches.

The number of plants that will thrive in complete shade, however, is more restricted. Yet such plants do exist and in numbers sufficient to bring colour and beauty to such difficult positions as a sunless north-facing border, or to lighten the gloom under dense trees or conifers.

Where perennials are concerned, there could be few better choices than the hellebores, a group of plants of which the Christmas and Lenten Roses are the best-known members.

Helleborus corsicus

Helleborus niger, the Christmas Rose, is one of the loveliest of winter-flowering plants, with its creamy-white chalices and striking boss of golden stamens.

To be certain of flowers at Christmas, as well as to protect the blooms from soil splashing, it is advisable to cover the plants with cloches. The variety Potter's Wheel needs no such protection since it holds its flowers high and comes into bloom early in December.

The Lenten Rose, *H. orientalis* and its hybrids, have a wider colour range – from creamy white through pink to deep maroon. These, as might be expected from their name, start to flower in mid-February, continuing until the end of April. Others which do well are *H. corsicus* and the green-leaved native hellebore *H. foetidus*.

For the dense shade under trees, the Oregon Grape, *Mahonia aquifolium*, is superb. In spite of these difficult conditions, it will still produce its yellow flowers in great profusion during February. The Butcher's Broom, *Ruscus aculeatus,* is another evergreen shrub that is equally accommodating. Its main attraction lies in its small assegai-like leaves.

Ivy, aucuba, privet and box all do well under trees and so, if the soil is lime-free, do rhododendron species, evergreen azaleas and camellias.

Mahonia aquifolium (*left*) and
Ruscus aculeatus

Westonbirt Dogwood

Wet soils

Drainage can be a problem on low-lying sites, especially where the soil is heavy clay. Anyone who gardens in these conditions will either have to put in some kind of drainage system or settle for growing the kind of plants that do not object to permanently soggy soil conditions.

In other gardens, too, there are sometimes damp marshy patches or a need for plants that will thrive in waterside conditions, on the margin of a stream or at the edge of a pool. Many attractive shrubs and perennials are happy in such situations and there are even a number that will flourish where the ground is more or less waterlogged.

For soils that are damp but not actually boggy, the astilbes are particularly useful. These striking perennials were illustrated on page 33.

Although day lilies will accommodate themselves to a wide variety of soil conditions, they are happiest where it is permanently damp. Here, their handsome clumps of sword-like foliage will spread with great rapidity, producing clusters of exotic trumpet flowers in great profusion and they are now obtainable in a great variety of colours and

Hippophae rhamnoides

flower forms. In addition to the orange and yellows of the older forms, the range now includes varieties with pink, apricot, salmon, scarlet and mahogany flowers.

Among the shrubs that take kindly to really wet soils are the mock oranges, or philadelphus, with their penetrating orange-blossom fragrance, weigelas of which the silver-variegated *W. florida variegata* is a particularly lovely form and the varieties of *Viburnum opulus*.

For really swampy conditions, Marsh Marigolds will make a bright splash of colour in spring. The double form, *Caltha palustris flore pleno,* is the best to grow. Here, too, the scarlet- and yellow-stemmed dogwoods will display their brilliant winter bark colouring to perfection. Of the former, the scarlet stems of the Westonbirt Dogwood are far and away the most eye-catching. The Sea Buckthorn, *Hippophae rhamnoides,* is one of the few berried shrubs that will tolerate swampy soils.

Caltha palustris

Seaside districts

Gardens by the sea present their own particular set of problems. Salt-laden winds can be injurious to many favourite plants that flourish elsewhere. There is, however, the benefit of a more equable climate, with milder winters and fewer extremes of temperature. Given protection from winds off the sea, a number of plants that, in inland areas, are tender or partially so, can be grown in the open with perfect safety.

Many grey- and silver-leaved shrubs flourish at the seaside including lavender, rosemary, *Olearia haastii,* with its grey, oval leaves and masses of white flowers and *Senecio laxifolius* with felted, silvery leaves and corymbs of yellow daisy flowers.

Tamarisks, too, with their deceptively delicate-looking, mimosa-like foliage, are never seen to better advantage than in seaside districts. *Tamarix pentandra* is the best flowering species, with lovely named forms like Pink Cascade, which throws up 6-ft. arching sprays, tipped with rosy-pink spikes of blossom. The flowering shoots of these shrubs should be cut back each spring, practically to their point of origin.

Escallonias are another race of seaside shrubs *par excellence* both for use as windbreaks and hedges and as specimens. Hybrids which are available include the crimson Donard Brilliance and Donard Beauty, the vivid red C.F. Ball and the delicate pink Apple Blossom.

Tamarix pentandra

Olearia haastii (*left*) and *Escallonia* Apple Blossom

For hedging, *Escallonia macrantha,* with rosy-crimson flowers and polished evergreen foliage, would make a good choice. Better still would be one of the larger-leaved forms of *Euonymus japonicus,* such as *E. j. macrophyllus* or the white-margined variety *E. j. albo-marginatus.*

Among the partially tender wall plants likely to thrive in maritime districts are the trachelospermums, with their heavily scented, jasmine-like blooms; the Potato Vine, *Solanum jasminoides* and the spectacular orange-red trumpet climber *Campsis tagliabuana* Mme Galen.

The various members of the dianthus family, including the pinks and carnations, all seem to flourish near the sea provided they are given, as well, the alkaline soil conditions they prefer. Roses, too, seem to give of their best.

On a sheltered wall, the passion flower, *Passiflora caerulea,* will produce its strange, striking flowers. Other partly tender shrubs, which would need the protection of a south wall in inland districts, can be grown quite safely in the open garden.

Rhododendron Pink Pearl

Lime-hating plants

Lime-hating plants have already been mentioned, but little has so far been said about the genus *rhododendron*, which includes in its ranks the brilliant deciduous and evergreen azaleas. Generally speaking, it is wasted effort to try and grow any of these, or other lime haters like the closely related Calico Bush, *Kalmia latifolia*, in alkaline soils, although some temporary measure of success may be achieved by planting them in extensive pockets or raised beds of peat. Some of the smaller rhododendrons and the lovely evergreen azaleas can also be grown successfully in tubs or other containers filled with a suitable acid growing medium.

However, for those soils with a pH factor of 7 or less rhododendrons and azaleas are practically a 'must'. Of the larger types, the superb hardy hybrids, with their magnificent evergreen foliage and large trusses of brilliant flowers, make the best choice.

All of these will flourish in full sun, provided that the site is well drained, fairly moist and rich in humus. Two of the finest named hybrids are the famous Pink Pearl and Mother of Pearl, both a delicate pink in bud, with flowers that turn to blush white as they open. Britannia, a showy red rhododendron of fairly dwarf habit; Mrs Furnival, soft pink blotched with wine red; and Susan, with lavender flowers verging on blue are other splendid varieties. Betty Wormald is another tried and true favourite with frilled pink flowers speckled at their throats, while Dairymaid and Harvest Moon are basically cream, with petals stained red at their base.

The deciduous azaleas are divided into several groups and the many lovely forms include the Mollis varieties and hybrids, which open their scented flowers before the leaves unfurl; Ghent hybrids, which are very fragrant and flower just as the leaves are opening, and the Knap Hill and Exbury Hybrids, both of which are noteworthy for the size, profusion and brilliance of their flowers.

The evergreen azaleas prefer a position in partial shade, although they will do well in full sun provided they are protected from cold winds. Hinodegiri, a brilliant, almost fluorescent red; Hatsugiri, a fine purple, and Vuyk's Scarlet are just three of the many outstanding named forms.

Kalmia latifolia

Evergreen azalea Hinodegiri

Chalk soils

The gardener on chalk is not at such a great disadvantage as one might imagine from the foregoing remarks. Provided that drainage is good and that the humus content of the soil is kept at a high level, the chalk garden can be persuaded to produce a great variety of worthwhile plants, some of which, in fact, are seen at their best in these conditions.

Perennials such as scabious and shrubs like the Wayfaring Tree, *Viburnum lantana*, holly, thorn and laurel, all of which are found growing on our chalk downs, point the way to the correct choice. Barberries and cotoneasters, too, do well on chalk.

Japanese cherries and flowering crabs are all happy on chalk soils, together with other ornamental trees like maples – with the exception of the Japanese varieties – laburnum, rowan and whitebeam. Many conifers, too, can be grown satisfactorily, including the magnificent cedars and deodars, cupressus, juniper, larch, pine and yew.

As a substitute for the colourful spring display of the deciduous azaleas, there are the brilliant tree peonies. Although they take longer than the former to reach their full flowering potential, they will provide a display that is equally worth having, once this point is reached.

Peonia suffruticosa, the Moutan or Tree Peony, is somewhat

Cotoneaster horizontalis

inaptly named, since it is shrub-like in character and seldom grows more than 6 ft. tall. Individual blooms can measure 6 in. or more across and an established plant can easily produce upwards of 50 flowers each season. There are single and double forms in a wide range of colours. Of the singles, Comtesse de Tudor, a pale shell pink, Lactea, a fine white with purple markings and striking golden anthers, and Osiris, a dark reddish-purple are all well worth growing. Good double forms include Elizabeth, salmon pink and Alice Harding, canary yellow.

Although they cannot produce the brilliant flowers of the hybrid rhododendrons, the so-called Japanese laurels, varieties of *Aucuba japonica,* can outrival the former in the beauty of their polished evergreen foliage. If male and female forms are grown together, there will be scarlet berries in autumn.

Other shrubs that flourish on chalk are the elegant evergreen *Azara microphylla,* with dark polished leaves and tiny, scented yellow flowers; the Judas Tree, *Cercis siliquastrum* and the Japanese quinces. Dogwoods, forsythias, lilacs, philadelphus, flowering currants, spiraea and viburnums are all ideal for growing on chalk and descriptions of all these have appeared on preceding pages.

Among the border plants that thrive in these conditions are scabious and all members of the dianthus family.

Dianthus x *allwoodii* (*left*) and *Scabiosa caucasica*

Rosemary (*above*) and lavender

Sandy soils

Sandy soils have one big advantage and that is that they are very easy to work at almost any season of the year. The main disadvantage is the speed with which fertilisers of any kind are leached by rain out of the soil, owing to its porous texture. The answer to this is to feed it with every scrap of organic material obtainable. If animal manures are not available use compost, peat, leafmould or, in seaside districts, seaweed, to step up the humus content of the soil.

Inorganic soluble fertilisers have only short-term value and it is better to employ organics like bonemeal and hoof and horn to increase the fertility of sandy soils.

Once a fertile soil has been successfully built up, a wide range of lovely plants can be grown. Among those that do particularly well are perenials such as thrift, sea holly, the globe thistles, rue, sedums, catmint and those accommodating grey- and silver-leaved shrubs that have so many garden uses: *Anaphalis triplinervis,* with its grey foliage and white everlasting flowers, artemisias, *Phlomis fruticosa* and *Lychnis flos-jovis*.

This applies also to grey-leaved herbs, such as lavender

and rosemary. In fact, all culinary herbs and their ornamental counterparts, with the exception of mint which prefers heavy moist soils, will thrive in dry, sandy conditions, including sage, thyme, bergamot and southernwood.

Brooms, gorses and heathers will all be in their element and in sandy gardens cytisus, genista and the golden-flowered Spanish Broom, *Spartium junceum,* with its rush-like foliage, should all be planted to provide colour from May to July. The Spanish Broom will in fact thrive almost anywhere and the large, fragrant flowers make it a very attractive shrub.

Genista hispanica, the Spanish Gorse, makes a compact spiny hummock that is smothered in yellow flowers in May. Two dwarf gorses, *Ulex gallii* and *U. minor* both flower in September and make an effective contrast to the regal purple of the summer heathers, varieties of *Calluna vulgaris.*

Trees and shrubs with pinnate leaves like laburnum, robinias and wisteria all seem to do their best on light sandy soils. The most striking robinia is the False Acacia (*Robinia pseudoacacia*) and the best variety of this is *frisia,* with foliage the colour of fresh-minted gold that turns to a pale lemon yellow in autumn.

Phlomis fruticosa

Ribes sanguineum

Clay soils

Once its potential fertility has been exploited, a clay soil can be one of the best for growing a great variety of plants successfully. Like sandy soil, but for different reasons, it should be constantly plied with material rich in humus. This opens up its sticky texture and when applied in sufficient quantities it helps to absorb any excess of moisture.

A clay soil should never be worked when it is wet and soggy or when it has dried out to a rock-hard consistency. This means that the best period for working these soils is restricted to a few weeks in spring and autumn and every opportunity should be seized to do this job when such suitable conditions exist. With newly dug plots it helps, too, if the soil can be thrown up in ridges during the winter so that wind and frost can break it down.

Although the great majority of popular shrubs will flourish in clay soils, once thay have been properly conditioned, there are quite a number that are not even averse to the sticky character of fresh-dug heavy clay soils.

Roses, of course, are well known for this tolerance, but

Pyracantha coccinea lalandii (*left*) and *Spiraea* Anthony Waterer

other shrubs, such as berberis, forsythia, philadelphus, lilac and dogwood all do well. Honeysuckle, kerria, pyracantha, ribes and viburnums can also be planted with every hope of success. Others that are equally popular and do well are hebes (shrubby veronicas), weigelas and *Corylus maxima atropurpurea*, a striking ornamental form of the hazels of our hedgerows.

Herbaceous borders on clay may pose difficult weed problems. Couch grass, dandelions and creeping buttercup are particularly troublesome – but perennials such as Michaelmas daisies, heleniums, erigerons, astilbes, delphiniums (but watch out for slugs), lupins, geums, peonies, phlox, sunflowers and shasta daisies all make a first-rate showing.

Among the ornamental trees suitable and compact enough for the small garden on clay are crabs, cherries, thorns and the golden-leaved alder, *Alnus incana aurea*.

Although this book does not cover the kitchen garden, it is worth pointing out here that a well-worked clay soil will grow the majority of vegetable crops, including beans and peas, to the peak of perfection.

CLIMBING AND WALL PLANTS

Walls, fences, pillars and pergolas can add what practically amounts to an extra dimension to the garden, in addition to providing opportunities for growing many slightly tender plants that would be at risk in the open garden. Many climbing plants are self-supporting. Ivies and Virginia creepers, for example, cling to walls and other surfaces by means of adventitious roots which spring from the stems and tiny sucker pads respectively. Others, like passion flowers, wisteria and clematis, support themselves by tendrils, twining stems or leaf stalks.

Wall shrubs like pyracantha and *Cotoneaster horizontalis* are not self-clinging but provided they are given a minimum of support and judicious pruning, they will mould themselves to the surface of the wall or fence on which they are growing. Others, such as climbing and rambler roses, camellias and the Winter Jasmine, will need tying in to the support.

Half-hardy climbers like the passion flower or the Potato Vine, *Solanum jasminoides*, will need the added protection of a south wall but the equally attractive climbing hydrangea, (*H. petiolaris*) and the Jew's Mallow (*Kerria japonica*) and all the ivies and Virginia creepers are perfectly at home on an inhospitable north wall.

A well-constructed trellis makes the neatest and longest-lasting means of support. The cross-battens should be mounted about 3 in. away from the wall surface to allow free circulation of air behind the plants. This is especially important where climbing plants such as roses, which are very susceptible to mildew, are concerned. Lengths of medium-gauge galvanised wire, stretched horizontally at 1-ft. intervals and attached to the wall surface by vine eyes, will provide adequate support for the majority of the twisters and twiners. With the more rampant climbers, such as wisteria and the more vigorous clematis species, plastic-covered wire-netting can be used.

Beds at the foot of the wall should be at least 18 in. wide. This gives the plants sufficient root run and eases the task of mulching and feeding. Where this is not practicable, that is where concrete or paving extends right up to the house walls, climbers can be grown in tubs or other suitable containers, although their growth will be much less prolific.

Wisteria on a pergola

Clematis montana rubra

North walls

Choosing climbers for a north wall is not such a difficult problem as it might at first seem. There are, in fact, some shrubs that are best grown in this situation, since their flowers are then less likely to suffer frost damage in spring.

Although camellias are completely hardy and will tolerate temperatures many degrees below zero, their lovely blossoms are extremely susceptible to damage by frost, both when the buds are showing colour and when the flowers are fully open.

Such damage is caused mainly by early morning sunshine after a hard night frost, resulting in too rapid a thaw which browns the petals and, in severe cases, causes the buds and flowers to drop. If a more gradual thaw can be arranged – and a position on a north wall provides for this – the risk of such damage is far less likely.

Among the loveliest and most free flowering of the camellias are varieties raised from the hybrid *C.* x *williamsii* of which Donation is the best known and most widely grown. It has exquisitely formed semi-double, peach-pink flowers, 3 to 4 in. across, with a striking central boss of golden stamens. Varieties of *C. japonica*, like the blood-red Adolphe Audusson, the rich crimson Donckelarii and the flesh-pink Lady Clare are also extremely well worth growing.

One of the most spectacular climbers for a north wall is the climbing hydrangea, *H. petiolaris*. This fully hardy shrub has all the virtues; self-clinging with large white panicles of blossom, it also has attractive foliage that turns guinea gold in autumn before it drops to reveal striking cinnamon twigs and branches in winter.

Shrubs which berry as freely on a north wall as elsewhere are worth finding room for. Striking examples of these are the firethorns or pyracanthas, as also are the wall-hugging species of cotoneaster, such as *C. horizontalis*, and *C. salicifolia*.

Ivy need not be drab and uninteresting if silver or gold variegated forms are planted. The large-leaved, yellow-margined *Hedera colchica dentata* is particularly striking. Clematis species, too, will be happy on the north and the lovely evergreen climbing rose Mermaid will produce its single golden blooms freely from July to November.

Climbing rose Mermaid (*above*) and *Hydrangea petiolaris*

South walls

The mellow warmth of a south wall should be reserved for the choicest climbers and wall shrubs and in particular for those partially tender subjects that are often among the most exotically beautiful of all garden plants. One such is the Lobster Claw or Parrot's Bill (*Clianthus puniceus*), with its polished pinnate foliage and striking bifurcated scarlet blooms that are responsible for its popular name.

The equally brilliant trumpet vine, *Campsis tagliabuana* also needs a south-facing wall to obtain maximum sunshine and protection.

Although the Winter Sweet, *Chimonanthus praecox,* does quite well in a sheltered position in the shrub border, it will flower earlier and more prolifically when afforded the shelter of a south wall. Planting this lovely winter shrub is in the nature of a long-term investment since it will not flower until it is well established. However, its intensely fragrant yellow flowers are well worth waiting a few years for.

Another shrub that benefits from this kind of protection is the Wire-netting Bush, *Corokia cotoneaster*. This is a tangle of

Campsis tagliabuana (*left*) and *Solanum jasminoides*

wire-thin twigs in winter which bear masses of yellow star flowers among the dainty leaves in spring. It lives up to its name in more senses than one since a mature plant can be used as a natural support for climbers of twining or clinging character.

Escallonias which, in colder districts, sometimes get cut to ground level or even killed outright when grown in the open will stand a greater chance of survival when grown as wall shrubs. All the varieties mentioned before can be grown successfully on the south of a house or on a south-facing wall or fence.

These, too, are the best positions for fruiting ornamental vines for although they are perfectly hardy, the small but very sweet grapes will stand a much better chance of ripening. The purple-leaved grape, *Vitis vinifera purpurea,* and the hybrid variety Brant both combine beauty and usefulness in full measure. Both will ripen their small black grapes on a sunny sheltered wall; both, too, have extremely decorative foliage – deep purple in the former – that assumes striking hues in autumn.

Clianthus puniceus

East and west walls

West walls have a slight edge over those facing in the opposite direction, but both are capable of supporting a host of delightful climbers. Given a cool, moist root run, clematis will succeed on any aspect but they are more likely to encounter the conditions that suit them best when they are grown facing east or west.

There are many lovely hybrid forms, but the more vigorous and easily grown species should not be neglected on their account. Particularly good on east walls are *C. montana* and *C. flammula* with thousands of tiny white flowers which scent the entire garden throughout August and September. *C. jouiniana* which has large clusters of soft lavender flowers together with the free-flowering garden varieties of *C. viticella,* the Travellers' Joy of our native hedgerows, are also very successful against east walls. All of these can hold their own with the more aristocratic hybrids of the Jackmanii, Lanuginosa or Patens groups.

The Tree Hollyhock, *Hibiscus syriacus*, is another fine shrub that is not as widely grown as it deserves to be. It makes a valuable late-flowering wall shrub, producing its hollyhock flowers in August and September. One of the best forms is Woodbridge, a large ruby-red single, while other varieties

Vitis cognetiae and *Chaenomeles* Knap Hill Scarlet

Wisteria sinensis

worthy of consideration include singles such as Hamabo and Blue Bird, blush pink and blue respectively, and the double lilac Souvenir de Charles Breton.

Honeysuckle and jasmine, two of the most fragrant of summer-flowering climbers, are also equally at home on an east or west wall. Both need plenty of wall space for their full development.

Jasminum officinale, the common jasmine, has masses of tiny white trumpet flowers, pink in bud, and with a penetrating fragrance. Of the honeysuckles, the Late Dutch, *Lonicera periclymenum serotina*, gets full marks for scent. *L. japonica aureo-reticulata,* on the other hand, is grown solely for the beauty of its foliage, which is delicately netted with gold.

Chaenomeles speciosa, the Japanese quince, seems happiest on the east. Knap Hill Scarlet, with terracotta flowers, is one of the best forms. Wisteria, on the other hand, favours the west. This majestic climber always looks best when it is grown with a single main stem, with laterals that are pruned back in summer and again in autumn, in the manner of cordon or espalier fruit trees. Some of the ornamental vines are equally attractive, particularly the flamboyant, giant-leaved *Vitis cognetiae*.

WATER PLANTS

A pool, whether formal or informal, natural or artificial, makes a delightful feature in almost any garden and a wide variety of plants can be grown in the merest trickle of water.

Most gardeners who construct a pool will want, first of all, to grow water-lilies. There are varieties that will thrive in shallow water and cramped conditions, but the choice will need to be made with care. More vigorous kinds would rapidly cover the entire surface of the pool, leaving little room for anything else.

For a pond of moderate size, around 2 to 3 ft. in depth, *Nymphaea* James Brydon has double crimson blooms of outstanding loveliness but there are even smaller varieties than this, suitable for the mini-pool or for planting in the shallows of larger water features.

Other suitable plants for a small pool are the Water Hawthorn, *Aponogeton distachyus,* with narrow, oval floating leaves and white, scented flowers; our native Water Violet, *Hottonia palustris,* whose pale yellow flowers break surface while the leaves stay submerged; the Common Arrowhead, *Sagittaria sagittifolia flore pleno,* with double white flowers; and the

Water-lily James Brydon

Lizard's Tail, *Saururus cernuus,* with creamy-white blossoms. All of these should be planted in shallow water, not more than about 4 in. deep.

There is also an attractive iris, *I. laevigata,* with flowers that are 5 in. across. There is a white form, *alba,* and *monstrosa* has violet falls that are creamy white at their base. There are, as well, the rich purple Regal, the dainty white Snowdrift and *elegantissina,* whose white-striped leaves and shapely, pale blue flowers make perfect partners.

Although the common bulrush is too large and too invasive for the shallows of a garden pool, there are two delightful miniatures – *Typha laxmannii,* whose chocolate-brown cats' tails are only 3 ft. tall and *T. minima,* which is even more compact, with a height of only 18 in.

Other attractive rushes for the water's edge are the Flowering Rush, *Butomus umbellatus,* and the Zebra Rush, *Scirpus tabernaemontani zebrinus,* grown for the unique beauty of its leaves which are banded horizontally with green and white.

Butomus umbellatus

BULBOUS PLANTS

When gardeners talk about bulbous plants, they generally stretch this term to include, as well, those that are grown from corms, rhizomes or tubers. Daffodils, snowdrops, hyacinths and lilies are all examples of bulbs; gladioli and crocus are corms. Rhizomes are fleshy underground roots by which plants like the bearded irises, montbretia and lilies-of-the-valley increase their numbers. Typical tuberous plants are the gay tuberous begonias, so useful for summer bedding, and the colourful ranunculuses, which are excellent for cutting as well as border decoration.

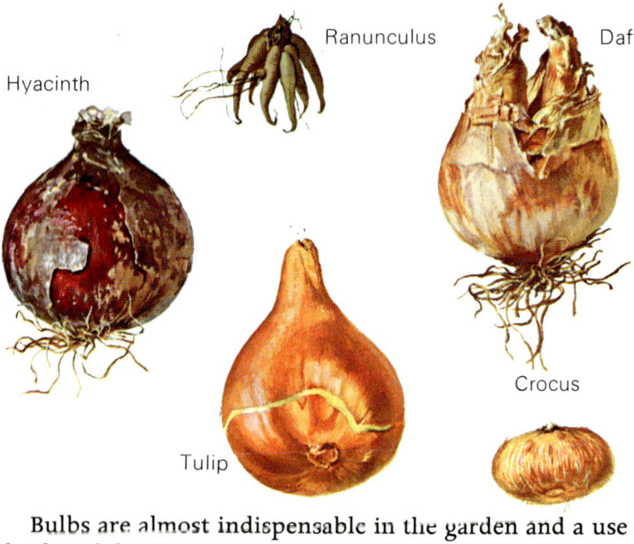

Bulbs are almost indispensable in the garden and a use can be found for them in every part of it. Daffodils, for example, never look better than when they are planted in drifts in the wild or woodland garden or grouped under shrubs or trees in the borders.

They can also be naturalised in grass, which can provide a delightfully Wordsworthian picture where the garden is large enough to include an area of rough grass such as an orchard or paddock.

Planting them in a formal lawn, however, is not the best of

ideas. The grass will have to remain uncut until the daffodil foliage has completely died down and in some seasons, this can hold up the first cut until well into June. This will do nothing to improve the texture of the lawn, quite apart from the untidy appearance.

The best place for bulbs in the small garden, apart from the use of tulips and hyacinths in spring bedding schemes, is in the shrub or mixed border. Here they can remain undisturbed for a number of years, until they eventually need lifting and dividing. It is advisable, before the foliage dies down, to mark

their positions in some way or some bulbs are liable to get spiked and damaged when the borders are being forked over in autumn.

We tend to think of bulbs as springtime plants, but there are many others that will continue to bring colour and beauty to the garden long after the last tulip has faded in early June. Lilies, of course, are among the loveliest of these, but there are others, flowering in summer and autumn, such as the Summer Hyacinth, *Galtonia candicans*, agapanthus, amaryllis, nerines and crinums.

Crocus tomasinianus

Early spring-flowering bulbs

We usually think of snowdrops as the first real harbingers of spring. In actual fact, however, it is the crocuses that come into flower first, with some species starting as early as September and continuing through November and December, until the better-known kinds start to bloom in February.

The first of the winter-flowering species is *C. laevigatus,* whose pale lilac flowers are banded with a deeper shade of the same colour. Also flowering before Christmas is *C. tomasinianus,* which naturalises freely in borders or in grass. Among the named forms whose colouring is an improvement on the rather washed-out blue of the species are Barr's Purple, with petals lined with greyish-mauve, Taplow Ruby, reddish-purple and Whitewell Purple, considered by most to be the finest and most free-flowering variety.

In late January or early February, the two species that provide the main display will be coming into flower. These are *C. imperati* and *C. chrysanthus*. Between them, they embrace all the lovely yellows, whites, lilacs and lavenders that brighten the last weeks of winter.

One of the loveliest sights of winter are the snowdrops. They naturalise well and once established will increase rapidly. The best kind for this purpose is *Galanthus nivalis*, the common snowdrop. Best results are obtained if growing bulbs are planted and there are specialist growers who will supply them in this condition in January and February. Dormant bulbs, planted in late summer or early autumn, will take longer to get properly established.

For planting in groups in the border, the giant snowdrop *G. elwesii* is a good choice. It flowers later than the common form, producing king-sized flowers on 12-in. stems.

One of the most reliable of winter-flowering subjects is the winter aconite with golden buttercup flowers, each surrounded by a ruff of bright green leaves, in January. Left undisturbed the winter aconites will increase rapidly, especially in moist soil conditions.

Snowdrop (*above*) and winter aconite

Narcissus bulbocodium conspicuus (*above*) and *Narcissus cyclamineus*

Spring-flowering bulbs

Daffodils

Daffodils are one of the most joyous sights in the garden each spring. To make their fullest decorative impact, they should be planted in groups, with one variety only in each. Six is the minimum number of bulbs that will make any appreciable effect but where space – and means – permit, groups of 100 or more would not be on too lavish a scale.

The following is a representative and worthwhile selection of the main categories which can be grown in a small garden.

Trumpet Varieties

Golden Harvest
Long yellow trumpet, deeply serrated.
King Alfred
Golden yellow – the most popular large-flowered variety.
Beersheba
Large pure white flowers on 2-ft. stems.
Mount Hood
White perianth with large ivory trumpet, fading to white.
Mrs E. H. Krelage
Best general purpose white.
Queen of Bicolors
Pure white perianth, canary yellow trumpet.

Large-cupped Varieties

Duke of Windsor
Broad white perianth, pale orange cup, edged with gold.
John Evelyn

Broad white perianth, frilled apricot cup.
Mrs R. O. Backhouse
The pink daffodil; creamy-white perianth, buff cup, tinged with pink.
Selma Lagerlof
White perianth, large frilled saucer-shaped, creamy-yellow cup, banded with white.
Fleurimont
Yellow perianth cup, tangerine orange merging to pastel orange.
Carlton
Vigorous and free flowering; large fluted yellow cup.

Doubles
Golden Ducat
Golden yellow, fully double.
Mary Copeland
Creamy white with centre of orange-red and yellow.
Texas
Gold and orange, early.

Miniatures
Peeping Tom
Cyclamen-flowered, lemon yellow with golden trumpets.
Yellow Hoop Petticoat
(*Narcissus bulbocodium conspicuus*) Bulbous yellow flowers aptly described by its popular name.
Rush-leaved daffodil (*N. juncifolius*)
Narrow rush-like leaves, yellow scented flowers.
Lent Lily (*N. pseudo-narcissus*)
Our dainty native wild daffodil.
Angel's Tears (*N. triandrus albus*)
Reflexed perianth, creamy-white flowers with globular cup.

Duke of Windsor (*above*) and King Alfred

Tulips

Flowering at the same time as the daffodils are a number of tulip species that provide a curtain raiser for the main display. As well as these, there are some early single and double varieties that can be used for bedding in March and early April.

The early-flowering tulip species are mainly dwarf in habit, flowering from March to mid-April. They look particularly effective planted in groups in the rock garden or at the edges of a shrub or mixed border.

Tulipa kaufmanniana, the water-lily tulip, flowers in March and contains some varieties of outstanding beauty. The pointed blooms, in an attractive range of colours, open out flat on sunny days, when they have a striking resemblance to the flowers from which they get their name.

Varieties include Shakespeare, whose colouring is a medley of salmon and orange; Stresa, whose petals are marked with red on the outside and black within, and The First which is carmine margined with white and ivory white inside. Heart's Delight is a lovely and unusual cherry-red tulip with a feathering of the same colour on the white edges of its petals, while Daylight is a vivid crimson-scarlet with the added attraction of leaves striped with cinnamon brown.

Among the larger early tulip species are the Lady Tulip, *T. clusiana,* and *T. fosteriana* Madame Lefeber, sometimes

Varieties of *Tulipa kaufmanniana*

Tulipa fosteriana Dance (*left*) and *Tulipa greigii* Corsage

listed as Red Emperor. Both of these have 15-in. stems which makes them ideal for early cut flowers. The Lady Tulip has small flowers, white outside and crimson within. Those of Madame Lefeber are much larger and a vivid scarlet in colour.

One of the smallest tulip species, ideally suited for the rock garden, is *T. tarda,* whose golden-yellow petals are tipped with white. It grows only 6 in. tall and flowers in early April.

The *greigii* hybrids are noteworthy for their unusual striped foliage and the brilliance of their colouring which, in many varieties, is enhanced by brown or black markings at the throats of the flowers. Among the most striking are the carmine and yellow Plaisir, the scarlet Red Riding Hood, the butter-yellow and carmine Yellow Dawn, and Pandour, which has faintly mottled leaves and subtle blend of rosy scarlet and cream in the flowers.

Darwin tulips for cutting

Following on the heels of the early tulips come the May-flowering or Cottage tulips. They are a little earlier than the Darwins as well as being more elegant, having blooms with pointed petals which are borne on tall stems.

Both the Cottage and Darwin varieties look well in mixed plantings and both kinds are superb for cutting. The bulbs should be planted 4 in. deep and 9 in. apart. Where very large numbers are being planted, a special bulb planting tool, which makes the hole and plants the bulb in one action, can be a great time and labour saver.

Mice are partial to tulip bulbs and a short length of rose pruning, or a sprig of holly, inserted in the soil to reach just above the noses of the bulbs will act as a deterrent.

There are many lovely named forms of Cottage and Darwin tulips; those mentioned here are purely a representative selection. Of the former type, Halcro is one of the best reds, with large and shapely carmine-red blooms that are a bright orange-scarlet on the inside of the petals. Palestrina combines salmon and rose pink to charming effect, whilst the flowers of Rosy Wings are salmon pink, with coral on the insides of the petals. There are some cheerful-looking yellows, including Asta Nielsen, lemon, Bond Street, buttercup, and Mrs John Scheepers, a fine variety with clear yellow flowers. White can be effective in massed plantings and Maureen is one of the loveliest of the whites.

Darwin tulips are the most widely planted of any and it is these that provide the bulk of the spring bedding displays. Only a few varieties can be mentioned here and a good selection would include Queen of the Bartigons, one of the loveliest pink tulips ever raised, La Tulipe Noire, a near approach to the mythical black tulip, Golden Hind, and that old pink favourite, Clara Butt.

There are also a number of unusual tulips, including some interesting hybrids. Best known of these are the Parrot Tulips with their waved and crested petals, interestingly flaked with contrasting colour. Fantasy, whose pink blooms are flecked with green, is one of the best known of these. There are also purple, scarlet and white forms, with similar striking characteristics. These flower late to provide an exciting finale to the tulip display.

Hyacinths

Although price-wise hyacinths are among the most expensive spring bulbs for bedding, they are well worth growing, as much for their uniformity and brilliance of colour as for the delightful perfume of their flowers. Planted under a sunny window, they will waft their glorious fragrance through the house. They also make excellent subjects for tubs or window-boxes.

Hyacinths look best in beds of a single variety, but if mixed beds are planted it will be advisable to make sure that the mixture consists of varieties that will flower simultaneously and it is worth while specifying this when ordering.

Hyacinths are traditionally associated with forget-me-nots, although the latter rather tend to distract from the finely chiselled beauty of the hyacinth blooms. Bulbs should be planted 4 to 6 in. deep and 5 in. apart. Ann May, rose pink; La Victoire, cerise pink; Delight, pale pink; L'Innocence, white, and Ostara, Oxford blue, are all good early varieties. They are closely followed into flower by Delft Blue; Lord Balfour, violet; Princess Irene, rose pink; and Salmonetta,

apricot. City of Haarlem, primrose yellow; King of the Blues, indigo, and Queen of the Pinks are three late-flowering hyacinths which will bring the season to a colourful close.

Beds for hyacinths and other bulbous bedding subjects should be prepared as soon as the summer bedding plants are out of the way in autumn. They should be dug over lightly, the surface soil being broken down to a fairly fine tilth with a fork. A dressing of well-rotted compost, fortified with bonemeal at the rate of $1\frac{1}{2}$ to 2 oz. to the sq. yd., should be sufficent to see the bulbs through their growing and flowering seasons.

In heavy soils, a sprinkling of silver sand in the planting holes before the bulbs go in helps to ensure good drainage and encourages rapid root formation.

After flowering, tulips and hyacinths can be lifted and transferred to a reserve bed, where they can remain until the leaves have died down. They will then be ready for digging up and storing until the following autumn when they should be planted out in their flowering positions again. Early autumn is the best time for lifting, dividing and replanting daffodils, just as the bulbs are starting to make their new root growth.

Hyacinths interplanted with forget-me-nots

Other spring-flowering bulbs

There are also a number of lesser-known bulbs that will greatly enhance the beauty of the garden in spring. One of the first of these to flower is the aptly named Glory of the Snow or chionodoxa. These make delightful little bulbous plants for the rock garden or they can be planted in groups in the shrub border. Here, they will soon form permanent colonies, provided they are allowed to remain undisturbed.

Chionodoxa luciliae has flowers of a clear Cambridge blue with a distinctive white eye. Those of *C. gigantea* are larger, and the blue petals are tinged with lavender. *C. sardensis* has the most striking flowers which rival those of the gentians in the intensity of their colouring.

Flowering later, with bell-shaped blossoms of an equally brilliant blue that make a perfect foil for daffodils, is the Siberian Squill, *Scilla siberica.* The small flowers, which are borne in clusters rather in the manner of those of Roman hyacinths, produce dazzling pools of colour. *S. bifolia* has stellate flowers of a deep sky blue that shade to a paler colour at their centres. *S. tubergeniana* has more restrained colouring

Fritillaria meleagris (*left*) and *Chionodoxa luciliae*

Iris reticulata

– a silver-blue faintly marked with a darker band through the centre of its petals.

It is not always the most flamboyant plants that give the greatest pleasure. The more modest charms of the Dog's-tooth Violet make it an ideal choice for a shady, moist spot in the rock garden. It only grows about 6 in. tall and flowers in April with nodding flowers, like miniature lilies, that are perfectly suited to the background of marbled leaves.

Another good plant for the rock garden that can also be successfully naturalised in grass is *Fritillaria meleagris*. The flowers are unique in being chequered like a draught board. The colour range tends to be subdued, but interesting, with slaty purples predominating. It has a much grander relation in the Crown Imperial, *F. imperialis,* whose ring of pendant bell flowers, yellow or orange in colour, are surmounted by a crown of spiky green leaves.

Summer-flowering bulbs

One of the cheapest, yet most striking of summer-flowering bulbs is the Summer Hyacinth, *Galtonia candicans.* The clusters of gleaming white bells, on their 4-ft. stems, look particularly fine in association with the tall blue spires of delphiniums. A native of South Africa, it likes a position in full sun.

The genus *allium* which contains the onions and leeks also sports some very lovely summer-flowering bulbs with spherical heads of bloom that look well in the garden and which also make attractive ingredients of summer flower arrangements both in bloom and dried, after the flowers have faded. *Allium moly,* the best known of these, has bright yellow flowers on 12-in. stems. *A. rosenbachianum* is a taller species with spectacular purple globes that are borne on stems 3 ft. or more in height. For the rock garden, there is a delightful 6-in. dwarf, *A. ostrowskianum,* with heads of carmine-pink bloom. However, the most outstanding of all the alliums is *A. giganteum,* a magnificent

Galtonia candicans

plant that lives up to its name. The stems are 4 ft. tall, surmounted by enormous globular heads of violet-tinged rosy blooms.

Agapanthus, with their large umbels of bright blue trumpet flowers, make an unforgettably lovely display in late summer. Most garden forms are slightly tender and need a sheltered position at the foot of a south wall. The Headbourne hybrids however, are said to be completely hardy.

Less eye-catching, but no less delightful, are the hardy autumn-flowering cyclamens, with blooms that are miniature replicas of the shuttlecock flowers of the indoor varieties. *C. europaeum* has crimson flowers that are sweetly scented whilst those of *C. neapolitanum* are rosy pink.

Splashes of bright colour are especially welcome in October and November and the Kaffir lily, *Schizostylis coccinea,* with its scarlet, gladiolus-like flower spikes, provides this in full measure. The bulbs should be planted in May, in a sunny bed or border.

Nerine bowdenii (*left*) and agapanthus

Lilies

Among the bulbs that flower in summer, lilies are in a class of their own. They have a reputation for being difficult to grow but this is almost completely undeserved. Most failures are due to one or more of three reasons – choosing species that are difficult to grow without careful treatment, planting bulbs that are damaged, diseased or insect infested or lack of sufficent soil preparation.

One of their main requirements is a deep, well-drained, fertile soil and wherever possible a position facing south. But since most lilies like to have their stems shaded, it is also advisable to plant them among shrubs.

Many lily species and hybrids will not tolerate lime; others are averse to acid soils. With the exception of *Lilium candidum*, which needs very shallow planting, the bulbs should be planted about two and a half times their own depth. Early autumn is the best time for planting. When planting is delayed until spring, some lilies may make no growth at all above ground during their first season.

Three of the easiest to grow are the Madonna, Regal and Tiger lilies. The first two are as noteworthy for their fragrance as for the beauty of their flowers. The trumpet flowers of the Madonna Lily are white, with striking golden stamens and each stem bears six or more flowers.

The Tiger Lily has brilliant orange flowers spotted with black and will naturalise freely if conditions are to its liking. The Regal Lily, *L. regale*, has pure white trumpets with golden-yellow throats and is one of the loveliest of all the lily species, rivalled only by the beauty of the Golden-rayed Lily of Japan, *L. auratum*. This species will not tolerate an alkaline soil but it can be satisfactorily grown in pots or tubs containing a suitable compost. Each satin-white petal of the glorious flowers is banded with gold and their fragrance will scent the entire area where the bulbs are growing.

In addition to the older favourites, there are now many exciting new strains of hybrid lilies. These include the Green and Black Dragon strains and the Preston, Backhouse and Bellingham hybrids. All of these have been developed and introduced with ease of cultivation in mind and most are both vigorous and disease resistant.

Lilium auratum
Lilium tigrinum
Lilium candidum

ORNAMENTAL TREES

It is, of course, no use even considering larger trees such as beech, horse chestnut, ash and others in the context of the small garden. Any of these would soon rob the surrounding soil of all nourishment and eventually create extensive areas of shade in which very few plants would flourish.

The ideal tree for the small garden is a multi-purpose kind; one, that is to say, that has more than one useful quality, such as beauty of blossom allied to good autumn leaf colour, decorative fruits or berries or beauty of winter bark.

It is dangerous, however, to plant trees even of moderate size too close to the house or other buildings since damage can be caused to drains or foundations by invasive roots. Some trees are worse than others in this connection and those with far-searching roots, like the poplars, should never be given a place in gardens of moderate size. In any case, trees should never be planted closer to the house than at a

Laburnum (*above*) and *Amelanchier canadensis*

distance equal to their ultimate height or spread, whichever is the greater.

Fastigiate trees provide a maximum effect in a minimum of ground space and one of the best of these is the Flagpole Cherry, *Prunus serrulata erecta* (syn. Amanogawa). This has the slender silhouette of a Lombardy Poplar, but grows only 15 to 20 ft. tall, with a spread of 5 to 6 ft. In April and May, this lovely Japanese cherry will be one of the finest sights in the garden – a close-packed column of scented pink blossom. The newer upright form of *P. sargentii,* Rancho, can be equally useful where space is restricted.

Another delightful small tree of upright habit is a variety of the False Acacia. *Robinia pseudoacacia fastigiata* has a slender pyramidal habit, elegant pinnate foliage and fragrant white flowers in June. The leaves turn a striking golden yellow in autumn.

Trees of weeping habit make ideal lawn specimens and Young's Weeping Birch, *Betula pendula youngii,* with its maxi-skirt of delicate twigs and lacy foliage is one of the loveliest of the small weepers. Delightful, too, particularly when they are in flower, are weeping cherries like Cheal's Weeping (*Prunus*

Magnolia soulangiana

Chamaecyparis lawsoniana wisselii

serrulata rosea) with double pink blossom that masses the branches in early spring. *P. subhirtella pendula* is another April-flowering cherry of more modest dimensions, with masses of pink flowers. There is also a weeping form of *P. yedoensis*, which opens its pale pink buds towards the end of March.

Among the other small trees suitable for the smaller garden are the ever popular laburnums. The hybrid *L. vossii,* with its foot-long golden tassels, is the most striking form. Other good specimen trees of modest dimensions include *Magnolia soulangiana,* with its white waxen blooms, the Snowy Mespilus, *Amelanchier canadensis,* which foams with white blossom in spring and blazes with brilliant leaf colour in autumn.

Where trees are concerned, proper planting procedure is of vital importance. In the early stages, full opportunity must be provided for the young fibrous roots to develop freely. Planting holes, therefore, whether in beds or in grass, must be both large and deep enough to allow these roots plenty of breathing space. In poor sandy soils or in very heavy clays, it will pay to remove all or part of the soil excavated from the planting hole, replacing it with well-rotted compost or a mixture of peat, loam and leafmould in equal proportions.

Where the garden soil is in good heart, peat or compost, enriched with a few handfuls of bonemeal, can be worked in round the roots when the tree is being planted.

Most trees, apart from a few like magnolias and arbutus that branch very close to ground level, will require staking. Stakes should be stout enough to support the tree for its first two or three seasons.

To avoid damaging the roots, it is better to get the stake in position in the hole before the tree is actually planted. The top of the stake should be just below the point where the main stem starts to fork. To avoid friction, the tree should be secured to the stake, using sacking and strong twine or one of the patent plastic or rubber tree ties sold specially for the purpose.

In gardens exposed to very strong winds a second stake, secured to the vertical one at an angle of 45 degrees, can be used to give a more wind-resistant support.

Tied to a bar of wood, a tree is easily positioned at the right depth. Stake before filling in

Padding at the tying point

Weeping cherry Shimidsu Sakura

Japanese cherries

The Japanese cherries are mainly varieties or hybrids of *Prunus serrulata*. To confuse the issue further, many have not only more than one Japanese name but conflicting Latin names as well. The cherry most widely planted is Kanzan, alias Hisakura, alias Sekiyama. This is a familiar sight in street and park plantings in all parts of the country. Kanzan is a vigorous grower, with semi-erect branches that spread out like a fan. To obtain its fullest impact, it should be viewed in the round and really needs more space than can be allocated to it in a garden of modest dimensions.

A more satisfactory choice would be one of the more compact varieties, such as Fugenzo (syn. *P. cerasus* James H. Veitch) with equally attractive double pink blossom. Fugenzo flowers late and for an early display it would be hard to better Hokusai (syn. *P. s. spiralis* and Udzu Zakura).

Of the whites, Shimidsu Sakura (syn *P. s.* Longpipes) and Shirofugen (*P. s. albo-rosea*) are both outstanding. Their flowers are pink at the bud stage, turning to white as they open. Shirofugen has beautifully bronzed young foliage while Shimidsu

Sakara, which flowers late, has distinctive fringed petals to its double flowers.

Ukon is unique among cherries in having blossom of a pale yellow. To enjoy its distinctive colouring to the full, Ukon should be planted in front of one of the pink or white varieties that is in flower at the same time.

In addition to the Japanese kinds there are several other prunus species that are well worth planting. For a plot with space to spare, our native Gean or wild cherry, *Prunus avium,* makes a handsome specimen tree, massed in April with delightful single white flowers. *P. serrula* is grown primarily for the attraction of its polished mahogany bark, while *P. subhirtella autumnalis* brings colourful blossom to the garden during any mild spells in autumn and winter.

P. maritima has really distinctive autumn leaf colouring. A deep coppery orange, with bronzed young foliage, this is one of the finest all-rounders producing its single pink flowers in March.

Prunus Kanzan (*left*) and *Prunus* Amanogawa

Crab apples John Downie (*above*) and Golden Hornet

Crab apples

Close rivals to the cherries in popularity and equal to them in decorative effect are the flowering crab apples, all members of the malus group. *Malus pumila* and its varieties have long been grown for their ornamental fruits, which also make excellent crab apple jelly. That old favourite John Downie is still one of the best for this latter purpose although there are others, like Golden Hornet, whose fruits are far more striking in appearance yet still make first-class jelly.

In the main, the blossom display of those varieties with decorative fruits is not as spectacular as that of kinds grown solely, or mainly, for beauty of blossom. Of the latter, those with purple foliage and deep red flowers are particularly worthwhile and this is a colour combination not found among the ornamental cherries. *Malus eleyi* Neville Copeman is one of the most outstanding of these, with soft pink flowers followed by large orange-red fruits.

Profusion is another comparatively recent introduction of the *M. lemoinei* type with masses of deep red flowers turning pinkish purple as they mature. The foliage is purple, tinged with bronze and the small fruits that follow the flowers are mahogany red.

One of the most sensational of all the flowering crabs is *Malus floribunda*, which rivals even the finest cherries in its beauty of form and profusion of bloom. In the species the flowers are deep carmine in bud, turning pink and finally white as they open. They cluster so thickly on the branches that the old saying about not being able to put a pin's point between them would be almost literally true. There is a variety *M. f. atrosanguinea* with a deep red bud that opens to a deep pink.

Among the most interesting introductions of recent years are the Canadian crabs. With these, we can enjoy the best of both worlds, since they have brilliant blossom followed by decorative fruits. Almay has maroon buds that open to paler flowers, starred with white at their centres; its orange fruits are small and flushed with red.

Cowichan is an early-flowering variety with rose-pink flowers and reddish-purple fruits. Its habit is broad and spreading. Simcoe is more upright in character, with large rose-pink blooms, coppery foliage and purplish-red fruits of a fair size.

Malus floribunda

SMALL TOWN GARDENS

Paved patios and terraces

In many instances, a town garden is scarcely more than an enclosed yard at the back or front of the house. Others are better endowed, with a plot of more reasonable dimensions, perhaps with the added advantage of a wall on either side. But whether large or small, a town garden can be transformed from a sooty wilderness into a minor miracle of beauty by treatment that is suitably inspired.

Underfoot, in the small town garden, paving is the best material. Wherever possible, natural stone should be used. Old York paving stones, once so readily obtainable from local councils at giveaway prices, but now incredibly expensive, are among the finest materials.

Beds can be left in the paving where the overall area is sufficient to warrant this, but since every square inch of space will be valuable, it may be preferable to grow the plants in tubs and other containers which can be moved about as required, with perhaps a narrow bed against the walls of the house for climbers.

Colour, of course, will play an important role, as it does in every other kind of garden. However, where the site is small

A paved patio with dwarf conifers, cotoneaster, thrift, helianthemums and ferns

and shaded by buildings, it may be necessary to rely mainly on foliage to provide such colour. Silver-leaved and variegated shrubs can look very effective in a partly shaded situation, while variegated ivies can provide even a north-facing wall with cheerful colour.

Apart from the plants grown in tubs, there will be opportunities to plant prostrate shrubs, conifers and perennials in the gaps between the paving. Several of the low-growing cotoneasters make useful subjects for this purpose. The best is *Cotoneaster dammeri* (syn. *C. humifusa*), which, once established, spreads rapidly, rooting as it goes, into every available crevice and cranny.

In autumn its stems will be thickly clustered with shining scarlet berries which, with luck, the birds will leave alone until well into the New Year.

There are, as well, a number of prostrate junipers that look well growing in paving. *Juniperus pfitzeriana*, the best known of these has, perhaps, too extensive a spread for the small town garden. It might be preferable to plant the slower-growing gold-leaved form, *aurea*. Other prostrate forms include *J. horizontalis,* with grey-green prickly foliage and *J. sabina tamariscifolia*, with soft, feathery spreading growths. The ultimate spread of these two will be between 6 and 8 ft.

Tub plants

A small patio or terrace in a town garden makes a perfect setting for plants in tubs, urns or the many other attractive kinds of plant container obtainable today. There is a choice to suit all tastes and pockets, ranging from antique urns and vases to more ordinary tubs of stone or wood. There are also some remarkably authentic-looking reproductions of lead urns, tubs and cisterns made of glassfibre and costing only a fraction of what their originals would.

Oak tubs make attractive and long-lasting containers, while wooden half barrels, painted white and banded with black make a more pleasing foil for plants in the town garden than the green ones more commonly encountered. Such containers should be treated with a non-toxic wood preservative before the plants go in. They must stand clear of the ground – on bricks or wooden blocks – to allow surplus water to drain away.

An advantage of tub gardening is that the containers can be moved around with the seasons to provide varying combinations of colour and form. The display need not be restricted to

Clipped box in a stone container

Hydrangea in a tub

summer although it is from June to September – the best season for sitting out of doors – that peak effects should be aimed at and this summer colour is easy to provide with bedding plants.

Spring bulbs will act as curtain raisers for the main display. Daffodils, hyacinths, tulips and smaller bulbs like scillas, chionodoxas and grape hyacinths all do well in tubs.

Shrubs can provide a more lasting and long-term effect. Varieties of *Hydrangea macrophylla* make especially fine flowering plants for tubs and by making it easy to provide the necessary acid soil conditions, we can be certain that the lovely blue varieties will come true to colour.

Even if the basic garden soil is alkaline, many of the lovely lime haters can be cultivated in tubs of acid peaty soil. Dwarf and medium-sized rhododendrons adapt themselves particularly well to this kind of cultivation.

Clipped box, bay or dwarf conifers all look well in tubs, box and bay lending themselves well to clipping.

Hanging baskets and window-boxes

Even where there is no garden at all, a great deal can be done to brighten up a town house or balcony flat by employing hanging baskets and window-boxes. Hanging baskets, obtainable from garden shops and hardware stores, are hemispherical in shape and made of stout galvanised wire.

Before filling them with a suitable growing compost, such as John Innes Potting Compost No. 2, the baskets must be lined. Sphagnum moss has for a long time been the accepted material to use for this purpose. Today, however, it is rapidly being replaced by polythene with holes slit for drainage.

Trailing plants make the most attractive subjects for hanging baskets. Trailing varieties of begonia and fuchsia, prostrate forms of lobelia, together with ivy-leaved pelargoniums, all make useful plants for the baskets in summer. A more permanent effect can be obtained by planting the baskets with hardy creeping plants such as the large- and small-leaved periwinkles (*Vinca major* and *V. minor*), Creeping Jenny (*Lysimachia nummularia*), ferns and variegated ivies.

Regular and careful attention to watering is important, especially where baskets are lined with moss. In these, evaporation will be more rapid. A liquid fertiliser applied at regular intervals will attend to the plants' needs nutritionally and guarantee a good show of bloom.

Window-box gardening can be a fascinating hobby for the flat dweller or for anyone else with limited space for a garden.

Miniature roses

Hanging basket with
pelargoniums and lobelia

Window-boxes, however, must be properly constructed to fit the ledge and should be firmly secured or they will be a distinct hazard to those who pass underneath them.

John Innes Potting Compost No. 3 makes a good growing medium. Alternatively, a mixture of 2 parts fibrous loam to 1 each of peat and sharp sand can be used. Careful planning should provide a long and colourful display from early spring to autumn. Early tulips could be followed by daffodils and hyacinths, while geraniums, scarlet salvias, petunias and other bedding plants would provide the summer display. These could be followed by chrysanthemums of the cascade or charm types.

For more permanent effects dwarf conifers, in association with some of the miniature roses mentioned on p. 129, could be planted. The latter include a number that grow no more than 6 in. in height as well as some that are perfect pygmy replicas of popular hybrid teas and floribundas.

ROSES

Roses play a part in the design of practically every garden. In a plot of limited size, however, it may not be possible to set aside an area for a rose garden proper. Wherever possible, however, hybrid teas and floribundas should be grown in beds apart from other shrubs and larger perennials.

Roses are one of the finest summer bedding plants and, in the long run, one of the least costly, since they are not discarded at the end of each season. Their flowering period is very long, lasting from June till October – and sometimes later – with only a few weeks' breathing space between the first and second flushes of bloom.

Although the hybrid teas produce the most perfect flowers, floribundas, generally speaking, give a better display as bedding plants. Their large clusters of bloom provide striking colour effects and among the newer introductions, known as grandifloras, there are many whose individual blooms have a perfection of shape that almost equals the hybrid teas.

Where space is insufficient for a separate rose garden or rose border, plants can be grown in the shrub or mixed border. The old-fashioned shrub roses make the best choice for this purpose and there are many delightful species and varieties. Unfortunately, many of these have only one comparatively short season of bloom each year.

Floribundas, too, are proving themselves very adaptable as plants to grow in association with shrubs. Their healthy constitutions and tremendous vigour enable them to compete on an equal footing with any but the most rampant growers.

Varieties suitable for the shrub border include the multicoloured Masquerade, with its harlequin medley of yellow, salmon and pink flowers at one and the same time; Chinatown, a tough and vigorous floribunda of great beauty; and the fantastic Queen Elizabeth, which makes a bush up to 10 ft. high and looks far more at home in the shrub border than towering above other roses in a mixed rose planting.

Among varieties more suitable for bedding are Dearest, a free-flowering salmon-pink floribunda, Elizabeth of Glamis, another fine salmon-pink rose, and the lovely red Rosemary Rose with flat blooms reminiscent of an old shrub rose.

A small rose garden

In recent years, the trend has been away from the more formal kind of rose garden towards a more natural employment of the 'queen of flowers' in the garden. Where there is room, however, there is no better setting for roses than in a separate feature of formal design, with circular, square or rectangular beds set among paths of grass, brick or natural stone, with pillars or pergolas to display some of the many lovely climbing and rambler roses.

A small pool with a fountain or figure makes an attractive focal point for a feature of this kind. Stone or wooden seats at suitable vantage points permit the enjoyment of the beauty and fragrance of the roses in greater comfort.

An open position, facing south or west, suits roses best. Grown in partial shade, the bushes tend to get leggy and flowers are borne less profusely. One place where roses should never be planted is under the overhang of trees as they will not tolerate drip.

Grouping for colour in a formal rose garden is important and although it may not always be practicable to have beds of a

Floribunda rose Frensham

single colour, which is the ideal arrangement, planting in blocks of six to a dozen plants of one colour produces an effect that is almost as satisfactory.

It is often claimed that roses do best in heavy clay soils. This is a fallacy. They require, above all, a well-drained soil and the ideal is a medium to heavy loam, rich in humus. Most types of soil, however, can be brought into a condition suitable for rose growing, provided that the drainage is satisfactory.

In both heavy and light soils, one of the first essentials is the provision of ample supplies of humus. This can take the form of well-rotted animal manure, leafmould, peat, spent hops or matured garden compost, the choice depending on whichever is the more readily available.

A dressing of bonemeal at the rate of 4 oz. to the sq. yd. will supply all the plants' other requirements during the first season after planting. Subsequently, the feeding programme will consist of annual winter applications of bonemeal, followed in spring by a topdressing of rotted manure or a good proprietary rose fertiliser, after the bushes have been pruned.

Masquerade (*left*) and Queen Elizabeth

Frau Karl Druschki as a standard

Standard roses are not as widely grown today as formerly but they can still be attractive as the central features of beds in a formal rose garden. Many of the popular hybrid teas and floribundas are obtainable in standard form. Among the best-known hybrid teas that are easily grown in this way are Ena Harkness, Fragrant Cloud, McGredy's Yellow, Peace, Piccadilly, Super Star and Wendy Cussons, and that really old favourite, Frau Karl Druschki. Floribundas that make good standards include Dearest, Elizabeth of Glamis, Iceberg, Masquerade and Orangeade.

Climbing roses, so invaluable for walls, pillars and pergolas are divided into several categories. The climbing sports of hybrid teas and floribundas have flowers that are identical with those of the corresponding bush varieties. Climbers seldom exceed more than 15 ft. in height.

It is advisable to leave these roses unpruned in their first season. Cutting back too hard at this stage will sometimes cause them to revert to bush habit. Among the best of the climbing sports are Climbing Etoile de Hollande, deep red, very fragrant; Climbing Mme

Caroline Testout, a fine old-fashioned pale pink cabbage rose, and Climbing Wendy Cussons, rosy red with paler reverse.

Perpetual-flowering climbers produce their blooms with great freedom over a long period. They are especially suited for pergolas. Danse du Feu, orange-red; Mermaid, single cream; Zéphirine Drouhin, the thornless rose, and New Dawn, shell pink, are some of the finest in this category.

Ramblers give a spectacular display of bloom for a few weeks around midsummer; after that, there is nothing. But the majority of rose lovers would not willingly forego the pleasure of growing them for this reason. Alberic Barbier, creamy white; Albertine, salmon pink; American Pillar, pink, with a white centre, and Paul's Scarlet Climber are all varieties of proven popularity for the better part of a century.

Miniature roses, not exceeding 6 to 12 in. in height, are ideal for the rock garden. Many are perfect miniatures of ordinary varieties; for example Baby Masquerade has all the characteristics of its taller relation. Another charming dwarf is *Rosa roulettii* which is a delicate pink.

The climbing rose Mme Caroline Testout

Planting: a new bush from the nursery with the old soil-mark at ground level

Pruning: An established bush

The best time for planting roses is in late autumn and in order to have the site properly prepared by that time, work should begin in mid-August or early September so that the soil has time to settle thoroughly before the roses go in.

They can also, if necessary, be planted at any time between November and the end of March, when weather conditions are suitable. However, with a spring planting they will require regular watering and frequent mulching during a dry spell.

In either case, the initial preparation of the site is a matter of the utmost importance to success. The top spit of soil must be thoroughly dug over and the subsoil should be broken up to another spade's depth. This is best achieved by taking out a trench, 9 to 10 in. deep and 18 in. wide, where digging commences and transferring the soil thus excavated to the opposite end of the site.

After breaking up the subsoil in the trench, the top spit of the next trench is used to fill in the first. This process continues until the site has been completely dug over when there should be an ultimate trench waiting to receive the soil from the first trench.

As digging proceeds, manure or compost should be worked into the lower spit, together with a dressing of superphosphate or bonemeal.

New roses should be planted $1\frac{1}{2}$ to 2 ft. apart, with the exception of particularly vigorous growers like Peace or Queen Elizabeth, which can be spaced $2\frac{1}{2}$ ft. apart. The planting holes should be both wide and deep enough to accommodate the roots without overcrowding.

Some of the soil from the planting holes can, with advantage, be replaced by a mixture of 4 parts peat to 1 of bonemeal, plus a sprinkling of hoof and horn. Alternatively, one of the proprietary planting composts could be used.

When planting, care should be taken to work soil well in and around the roots, afterwards firming them thoroughly to ensure that no air pockets are left.

New bushes can be pruned before they go in. All damaged roots and shoots should be cut back to sound material. Main stems can be shortened to four or five buds, if the nursery has not already done this prior to dispatch, and any dead or diseased shoots must be cut right out.

Pruning: First, all weak growths and old dead wood must be removed

Pruning: All long healthy growths are shortened back leaving a neatly shaped bush with ample space between the shoots

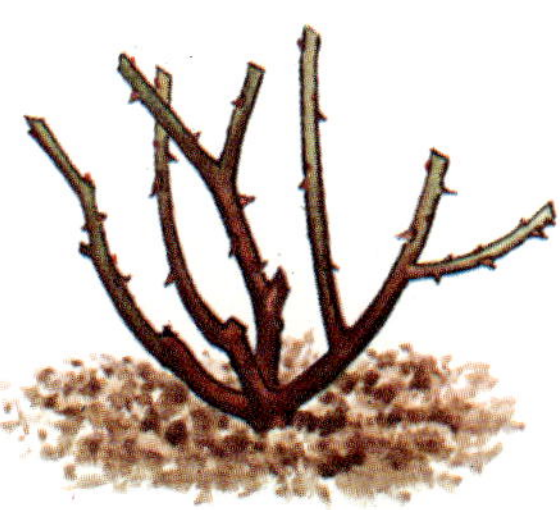

Roses, more than most garden plants, are susceptible to attack from a large number of pests and diseases.

The three major fungus diseases to which roses are prone are rose mildew, black spot and rust. The first of these makes the bushes look unsightly, but does not seem to cause any permanent damage. A regular spraying programme with dinocap beginning in mid-July and continuing until mid-September, provides the best answer.

Black spot can have more serious consequences and the initial symptoms take the form of small black dots on the leaves which later develop into circular black or dark purple spots

Black spot

Rose rust

Damage by leaf-rolling sawfly

that eventually cover the entire leaf surface. Spray with captan or maneb as soon as the young shoots start to unfurl and continue to spray at regular intervals.

Rust is the most deadly of the fungus diseases affecting roses. The disease first makes its presence felt in early spring in the form of small yellow pinhead swellings on the undersurfaces of the leaves. They later turn bright yellow, eventually becoming black and causing premature leaf fall. Finally, the disease spreads to the stems and dormant buds. A colloidal copper spray, applied from the end of May onwards, prevents an attack from reaching serious proportions.

Aphids or greenflies can cause considerable damage to young growths and flower buds. They can be controlled with derris dusts or sprays which are also effective against the other rose pests named here and have the added advantage of being completely non-toxic to humans and animals. Systemic insecticides are also being increasingly used.

Other serious pests include the caterpillars of the tortrix moth and the larvae of the leaf-rolling sawfly. Both attack

Rose leaf-hopper damage

Powdery mildew

Greenfly

young foliage and flower buds and both make use of the leaves as a protective covering. The most effective cure is to pick off and burn all affected foliage.

Thrips can cause much damage and disfigurement of young shoots and flower buds. Applications of derris should start well before the flower buds start to open.

Other pests, less common, but very harmful in some seasons are rose leaf-hoppers, chafer beetles and the leaf cutting bee.

FLOWERS FOR CUTTING

Annuals

Wherever possible, part of the garden should be set aside for growing flowers for cutting. This will avoid the beds and borders being decimated, although, fortunately, the majority of annuals seem to thrive on cutting and a policy of 'cut-and-come-again' will only serve to prolong their flowering season.

Sweet peas are one of the most valuable of all annuals for cutting. Whether they are grown on the cordon system or are allowed to develop naturally on tall, twiggy pea-sticks, they will continue to flower the whole summer through, provided that spent blooms are removed regularly and that the plants are not allowed to set seed.

Thc introduction of the dwarf Knee Hi and other similar strains has made it possible for even the smallest garden to grow its quota of sweet peas, since these need only a minimum of space and staking.

Seed should be sown in boxes in a cold frame or cool greenhouse at the end of September. When they are large enough to handle, the seedlings are transferred to thumb pots and over-wintered in a cold frame. They should be planted out in their permanent positions in late March or early April.

Everyone will have his favourites, according to whether the flowers are required for exhibition, cutting, fragrance or garden display. Some varieties combine all these qualities and mention should be made of the blue Noel Sutton, which has fragrance, great vigour, flower size and length of stem, all to a marked degree.

Other easy-to-grow annuals and perennials from seed especially prized by the flower arrangers include *Achillea filipendulina* with its yellow, plate-like heads that can be dried for winter arrangements, the Lady's Mantle, *Alchemilla mollis* whose lime-green feather flowers associate so well with the old-fashioned shrub roses, dwarf belladonna delphiniums and annual larkspurs; spurges, both annual and perennial, the long-tasselled love-lies-bleeding, especially the unusual green form, Bells of Ireland, (*Molucella laevis*) and the lovely new Sensation strain of nicotiana whose flowers, unlike those of the older kinds, remain open in the daytime.

Untrained sweet peas on sticks

Cordon method

Perennials

Because each individual plant, or group of plants, adds its decorative quota to the overall effect of a herbaceous border, it would be unwise to cut their flowers too freely for the house. Unlike annuals, most perennials have a limited flowering season and cutting will seldom do anything to stimulate the production of fresh blooms.

It can, however, be practised in moderation, especially from such plants as heleniums, Michaelmas daisies and golden rod, which provide a lavish supply of blooms. An alternative would be to grow a few rows of mixed perennials specifically for cutting, in the vegetable plot or in an odd corner of the garden.

Many perennials have either woody or hollow stems so that extra care will be necessary to prevent premature wilting. All flowers should be gathered in the early morning or late evening and they should be given a good drink overnight or for three or four hours before use.

Among those that are most accommodating are the herbaceous peonies. These can be gathered when the buds are first starting to show colour. They open in water to perfect blooms which will remain attractive for several weeks.

Of other perennials that flower in early summer, lupins, especially the Russell strain with their bold, full flower spikes, together with the globe flowers, pyrethrums – with their single and double daisy flowers – and the stately spires of delphiniums all make magnificent cutting material. Where the last named are concerned, however, the 6-ft. spikes of the taller varieties may prove somewhat overpowering for the average room. The belladonna types, which grow only 3 ft. tall, are much more satisfactory. Pink Sensation, with its long flowering period, is particularly lovely in this connection.

Later in the year, there will be the pure white flowers of the shasta daisies. One of the finest of these for cutting is H. Siebert, whose large single flowers have attractively fringed petals. Everest is the best of the more conventional singles and there are also a number of fine double varieties.

The tall spikes of *Acanthus mollis* with their lilac-pink hooded flowers will add a touch of drama to large arrangements. Other perennials that cut well include the taller campanulas, hellebores, eryngiums or sea hollies, day lilies, bearded irises and phlox.

An arrangement of herbaceous peonies

Flower arrangers set great store, as well, by foliage, choosing it with care for its beauty of form, texture or colouring. Beautiful leaves are no less valuable in the garden, especially when the tide of flower colour is at a low ebb.

Some perennials are as much worth growing for their foliage as for their flowers. By including them in the perennial border, one can greatly extend its period of interest and, in the case of evergreen perennials, this will continue into winter.

Bergenias are a good example of the last named. Their evergreen leaves are large and fleshy, eye-catching in winter and summer alike. Of the numerous species and hybrids, several

Hosta sieboldiana

are particularly deserving of a prominent place in the garden. Ballawley Hybrid has leaves that turn a coppery red in winter and produces large trusses of crimson flowers in early spring. Evening Glow has spikes of reddish-purple flowers in April and May. Silvery Light, whose white flowers have contrasting calyces of a delicate pink, is one of the loveliest and most unusual of the hybrid bergenias.

Another fine family of evergreen perennials are the acanthuses. There are two well-known garden species, *Acanthus mollis*, with broad shining lobed leaves and *A. spinosus*, which has spiny, thistle-like leaves.

Hostas are grown primarily for the beauty of their bold foliage. The flower spikes, white, pink, lilac or mauve according to variety, are a welcome extra attraction.

Of the hostas, none is more striking than *Hosta sieboldiana glauca*, with its enormous blue-grey, plantain-like leaves, 9 in. in width and half as long again. There are also some interesting and worthwhile smaller-leaved species and varieties with silver, cream or gold variegation. These should not be omitted from any representative collection. Thomas Hogg, whose broad leaves are edged with white, and *H. fortunei albopicta*, with scrolled leaves of butter yellow and pale green, are both especially worth growing.

Flower arrangers are particularly fond of grey-leaved plants and the hardy eucalyptus, *E. gunnii*, is one of their favourites. The grey-green Lady's Mantle, *Alchemilla mollis*, makes a perfect foil for the beauty of old-fashioned shrub roses.

Eucalyptus gunnii and *Alchemilla mollis*

Shrubs

It is not generally realised what a large amount of cutting material can be provided by flowering shrubs. Usually, however, it will be necessary to wait until our shrubs come to maturity before we can help ourselves lavishly to their blossoms. But those like the Winter Jasmine that flower on their current season's wood can, of course, be cut without any qualms, since this will be anticipating the correct pruning procedure by only a few weeks. Others, such as camellias, azaleas and magnolias are so slow growing that for many years we shall be unable to do more than sample their lovely blossom.

In winter, good cutting material is provided by shrubs such as *Viburnum fragrans,* Winter Sweet and Witch Hazel, together with the Cowslip Bush, *Corylopsis spicata,* and the hyacinth-scented *Daphne mezereum*. Later, forsythias, flowering currants, spiraeas, brooms, lilacs, escallonias and philadelphus all make their colourful contributions.

Established rhododendrons and azaleas are a rich source of cutting material. The flowers can be picked while still in bud and will open and last for as much as a fortnight in water.

From midsummer onwards hydrangeas, with their colourful and long-lasting qualities, will furnish the flower arranger with plenty of fresh and potential dried material. As well as the large mop heads of varieties of *Hydrangea macrophylla,* which look too artificial for some people's tastes, there are the shapely off-white flower trusses of the bone-hardy *H. paniculata grandiflora*. These become attractively tinged with carmine pink as they mature.

The blooms of *H. macrophylla,* however, are second to none for winter use in dried arrangements. There can be few other flowers that retain so well their original beauty of form and colour after being subjected to a drying process.

The method used for hydrangeas is to pick the blooms as soon as they are fully open and place them in a deep container of water, which should reach at least half way up their stems. They are left until the water has evaporated and can then be tied in bunches and hung up, heads downwards, in a dry airy shed or garage until they are required for use.

Shrubs as cut flowers: escallonia and philadelphus

Shrubs, as well, provide a wealth of useful foliage for cutting. It takes a number of contrasting forms and textures, ranging from the silver leaves of *Convolvulus cneorum* to the handsome green and gold of the wild olive, *Elaeagnus pungens maculata*.

Many variegated shrubs are grown almost solely for the beauty of their foliage and most of them cut well. This is true of *Cornus alba sibirica variegata,* whose leaves are a medley of soft green and silver and whose elegant sprays of foliage are first rate for cutting. There are also attractive variegated forms of *Cornus mas* and *Weigela florida*.

Variegated hollies are greatly in demand for Christmas decorations and arrangements, but to enjoy their varied colourings to the full, they should be given a position in full sun. Golden King, green leaves edged with gold; Golden Milkmaid, gold with a narrow margin of green; and Madame Briot, gold blotched with green, are all outstanding forms of the common holly, *Ilex aquifolium*.

The foliage of evergreen shrubs is naturally long lasting when cut. If this characteristic is allied to beauty of leaf texture, as it so often is, they will make ideal cutting material for the house vases. *Choisya ternata,* the Mexican Orange, has glossy

Fatsia japonica leaf (*left*) and *Elaeagnus pungens aurea variegata*

three-fingered leaves and is one of the finest foliage shrubs for alkaline soils. All the mahonias, including the magnificent *M. bealei, M. lomariifolia* and the hybrid Charity, would be well worth growing for the beauty of their leaves alone but they have an added bonus in their flowers and berries.

We seldom think of rhododendrons as foliage plants, but some of the larger-leaved species are outstanding in this respect. In some, such as *R. sinogrande,* the leaves are 2½ ft. in length and 1 ft. wide. *R. sinogrande,* in fact, has the largest leaves of all the hardy shrubs in cultivation in this country, but those of other species, such as *R. fictolacteum* and *R. basilicum,* are hardly less noteworthy. The large leathery bottle-green leaves of the former species are felted with cinnamon on their reverse.

The False Castor Oil Plant, *Fatsia japonica,* is a shrub that is very dear to the flower arrangers on account of the long-lasting qualities of its evergreen palmate foliage. It lasts for weeks in water and will flourish and flower on the most inhospitable of northerly aspects.

Rue (*Ruta graveolens*) makes a good small foliage shrub, especially the variety Jackman's Blue.

Mahonia bealei (*left*) and *Ruta graveolens* Jackman's Blue

CONIFERS

Conifers, apart from all their other virtues, are invaluable in providing year-long interest and colour that is unrivalled even by the evergreens. The dictionary definition of a conifer is 'a tree bearing cones composed of bracts which shelter the unenclosed seeds' and although the cones of some species are impressive conifers are mainly grown for their beauty of architectural form and the colour and texture of their foliage.

Most conifers are evergreen, but there are certain exceptions, including all the members of the larch family, the Maidenhair Tree, *Ginkgo biloba,* and the so-called 'living fossil', *Metasequoia glyptostroboides.* They take many different forms – fastigiate, umbrella shaped, spreading, creeping and weeping being just a few of them.

There are conifers to suit every type of garden, ranging from stalwart one-hundred footers to dwarfs only a few inches high. The vast majority will flourish in a wide variety of soils, apart from poor chalky land, pure sand or very acid peat.

The most widely grown group of conifers are the cypresses, which we used to lump under the botanical name of *Cupressus,* but which have now been split up, the majority having been hived off under the generic title of *Chamaecyparis.*

Many of the most useful garden conifers are found among varieties of Lawson's Cypress, *Chamaecyparis lawsoniana.* The

Juniperus pfitzeriana

species makes a tall, pyramidal tree, while its many lovely named varieties range from pygmy conifers to very tall specimens.

For the smaller garden, the best choice would be those varieties of compact and upright habit that do not exceed 20 to 30 ft. in height at maturity. *C. l. fletcheri* is one of the most popular of these. It makes a close-packed pyramid of glaucous-blue, feathery foliage. That of *fraseri*, a conifer of slender, spire-like habit, is grey-green. Green Pillar, a variety of *C. l. erecta*, is noteworthy for the rich green of its foliage and the perfect symmetry of its conical form.

Golden conifers are especially attractive, giving as they do an illusion of sunshine on

Chamaecyparis lawsoniana columnaris

Chamaecyparis obtusa nana pyramidalis

the dullest of winter days. Two outstanding varieties of *C. lawsoniana* are *lutea,* which will ultimately exceed the 30-ft. limit and *lanei,* which is broader based and more spreading than the former.

The choicest golden conifer of all belongs to a different species. This is *C. obtusa crippsii,* which is very slow growing but which will eventually attain a height of around 30 ft. Its foliage is the colour of a newly minted sovereign and its habit is broadly pyramidal. *Crippsii,* incidentally, has a preference for rather moist conditions.

The junipers are another race of conifers that provide a rich source of garden material. The best known is the Irish Juniper, *Juniperus communis hibernica,* which has a pencil-slim column between 10 and 15 ft. tall, but only about 18 in. in diameter. This makes an excellent specimen for a formal setting.

The variety *pfitzeriana* has already been mentioned in connection with paved gardens. Its tiered, spreading branches associate well with the low, uncluttered lines of contemporary one-storey buildings. There are forms with gold or blue-grey foliage, *aurea* and *glauca* respectively, while the variety *compacta* more than lives up to its name: it can take as long as 10 years to reach a height of 3 ft. and attain a 6-ft. spread.

Where there is space on a lawn for a large specimen conifer, none could produce a more magnificent picture than one of the stately cedars. But even the smallest of them, the Himalayan Cedar, *Cedrus deodara,* has a spread of between 30 and 40 ft. while the even lovelier Blue Cedar, *Cedrus atlantica glauca,* needs double that amount of elbow room.

It may seem surprising to some that yews should come into the category of conifers. In actual fact, the English Yew, *Taxus baccata,* is one of our three native conifers. The other two are the Irish Juniper and the Scots Pine.

Although the common form of yew is well suited to hedging and topiary work, fastigiate forms, with either dark green or gold-variegated foliage, make much more attractive specimens. These will grow, very slowly indeed, to an ultimate height of around 15 ft.

For the gardener with a mini-plot, there could be few more useful and interesting subjects than dwarf conifers. However, to grow them requires a patient disposition. Many take 10

Ginkgo biloba

Taxus baccata fastigiata

Juniperus communis hibernica

A sink garden

years or longer to reach maturity. There are, however, so many attractive and unusual kinds that results are well worth waiting for.

Lawson's Cypress, already mentioned, includes among its many varieties a number of delightful dwarfs with the typical broad-based pyramidal habit of their larger relations. *Chamaecyparis lawsoniana nana,* for example, develops slowly into a chunky cone of rich green foliage a foot or so in height. *C. l. minima,* an even more compact form, has vertical main stems with side branches set at right angles to give an interesting edge-on view of the foliage. There is also a fine golden form, *minima aurea,* as well as one with blue-grey foliage, *minima glauca.*

Others differ greatly in character from the orthodox conical shape. *C. l. nidiformis* has bluish-green foliage and an arching habit of growth. *C. obtusa pygmaea* is a flat-topped miniature with fan-shaped foliage that is tipped with bronze in winter.

The *pisifera* species, formerly known as retinisporas, have a more feathery type of foliage, especially where young growth is concerned. *C. p. plumosa compressa,* which likes partial shade, forms a tight little cushion of soft green, gold-speckled foliage.

The junipers, too, include one exquisite miniature whose slim columns make it a good focal plant in the rock or heath garden. This is *Juniperus communis compressa,* with blue-grey slender columns that seldom exceed 2 ft. in height. It is extremely slow growing.

One of the most fascinating of these dwarf conifers is a pygmy relation of the Christmas Tree, a tiny spruce known as *Picea abies nidiformis.* This is a spreading mass of closely needled branches, with a flat, indented top, the reason for its popular name of Bird's Nest Spruce. The stately Scots Pine can be represented in the rock garden by a perfect miniature, only 4 to 5 ft. in height. *Pinus sylvestris beauvronensis* has short branches, close packed with needles of a lovely greenish blue.

I have mentioned above how *Juniperus communis compressa* can be used as a focal plant. It is worth noting that other dwarf conifers can also be used for special effects in group plantings, especially when they have distinctive shapes or spread a low green carpet among other colours.

FERNS

Our Victorian forebears had a great liking for ferns and many of their gardens or conservatories included a feature known as a 'fernery'. With the present-day interest in shade-loving plants, ferns, for many years almost completely ignored by gardeners, are enjoying a renewed burst of popularity.

There could be few more easily grown plants for shady banks and borders and many of the smaller kinds make useful subjects for the northern slopes of a rock or heath garden.

Hardy ferns will succeed in almost any kind of soil conditions although the majestic Royal Fern, *Osmunda regalis,* does not like alkaline soils. Most, however, are seen at their best in a cool moist situation. Many are natives of Britain and the Hart's Tongue, Male and Lady Ferns can be seen growing wild in our woods and shady hedgerows.

A rarer native is the Maidenhair Fern, *Adiantum capillus veneris,* with its jet-black stems and lacy green foliage. This is a rather tender fern and in the colder parts of the country it would be safer to plant *A. pedatum* or *A. venustum,* both of

Asplenium felix-femina (*left*) and *Osmunda regalis*

Blechnum spicant

which have the typical lacy foliage of the Maidenhair Fern itself.

Both the Male Fern, *Dryopteris filix mas*, and the Lady Fern, *Athyrium filix-femina*, are completely hardy. Once established, the Male Fern will spread rapidly to provide good ground cover. It is particularly beautiful in late spring when green and russet can be seen in a perfect combination. The Lady Fern is similar in general outline, but its foliage has a lacier, more delicate texture.

The Royal Fern, which has now been included in the list of protected British wild plants, is one of the handsomest of our native ferns, reaching a height of up to 6 ft. in moist, almost boggy soil conditions.

More compact but equally distinctive is the evergreen *Blechnum tabulare*. The finely divided fronds are dark green and leathery in texture. It will quickly spread, by means of underground roots, to form extensive clumps. In cold districts, both this fern and the adiantums should be protected with a covering of straw or bracken during the winter.

ORNAMENTAL GRASSES

The gardener with a liking for fine foliage plants can find many uses for ornamental grasses in the garden. The taller kinds make good dot plants for focal points in the herbaceous or mixed border, while the smaller species are excellent as permanent edging plants for summer bedding schemes. Many, too, are grown for the decorative quality of their flowers.

Both the hardy and half-hardy annual grasses are easy to grow from seed. Cloud Grass, *Agrostis nebulosa,* and Annual Quaking Grass, *Briza maxima,* are both hardy annuals that can be sown out of doors in spring, where the plants are to grow. The former has misty-looking sprays of flower; quaking grass produces nodding white scaly blooms on wire-thin stems that look rather like miniature Chinese lanterns.

Two half-hardy annuals that are good for cutting are *Pennisetum villosum,* an elegant grass with arching leaves and stems that bear 6-in. long feathery plumes, and a culti-

Miscanthus sinensis (above) and *Phalaris arundinacea picta*

vated variety of the Foxtail Millet, *Setaris italica,* with nodding sprays of yellowish-green flowers.

One of the most popular of the perennial grasses is *Phalaris arundinacea picta,* better known as Ribbon Grass or Gardener's Garters. Ribbon Grass spreads rapidly by means of underground stolons and needs positioning with care.

Where a more compact plant is required, it would be better to plant *Miscanthus sinensis,* a handsome grass that grows about 6 ft. tall. The narrow leaves of the species have a white central vein and there are also forms with cream or golden-yellow variegation.

One of the best dwarf edging grasses is a variety of Sheep's Fescue known as *Festuca ovina glauca,* or Blue Grass. This makes dense blue-grey tufted clumps about 9 in. high.

The aristocrat among grasses is undoubtedly the Pampas Grass, *Cortaderia argentea,* whose stately 8-ft. clumps make such admirable lawn specimens. To ensure success plant in April.

Cortaderia argentea

BAMBOOS

Bamboos are closely related to grasses although they are comparative newcomers to our gardens. They have a decided preference for rich moist loams, so when grown on lighter soils they should be provided with adequate supplies of humus. They often take several years to establish themselves and for the first few seasons after planting it is advisable to mulch the young clumps generously.

In seaside districts, where mild moist air simulates the conditions of their native habitat, bamboos do particularly well and they are ideally suited for waterside plantings.

Early autumn and late spring are the best times for planting, although division of existing clumps is often most successful if delayed until May or early June, provided that the plants remain out of the ground for the shortest possible time.

Arundinaria japonica is the so-called Metake or Female Bamboo. Its erect canes, gracefully arched at their tips, grow 12 ft. tall. *A. simoni* is another vigorous and rapid grower with canes that will sometimes top 20 ft. But both of these are dwarfed by *A. fastuosa,* whose erect dark green shoots sometimes reach a height of as much as 25 ft.

A. nitida and *A. murielae* are both species that combine beauty and hardiness. The canes of the former are deep purple, with small leaves borne as plumes of vivid green. The slender shoots of *A. murielae* are enhanced by elegant foliage of a softer green. Both of these grow about 8 ft. tall.

Phyllostachys flexuosa makes a compact clump of arching growth to about 8 ft.; the canes of *P. nigra,* green at first, but turning black as they come to maturity, are complemented by the dark green foliage. *P. viridi-glaucescens* has decorative yellowish-green canes, ringed with purple at the joints.

Here then are some but, by no manner of means all, the plants that the gardener with a small plot can use to paint his own individual garden picture. I would stress once again the importance of choosing plants to suit existing conditions of soil and situation. This, in the long run, is the only true way to successful and trouble-free gardening.

One thing is certain. Nobody could possibly complain that his choice of plants is restricted.

Arundinaria japonica
Arundinaria nitida

The months and seasons mentioned in this book apply to temperate regions of the northern hemisphere (Europe, Canada and the northern United States). For readers living in other regions, the following table gives approximate equivalents.

Subtropical regions of the northern hemisphere (Mediterranean Sea, southern United States)
Plants will tend to shoot and flower a month or so earlier in these regions.

Tropical regions (around the equator)
No seasons exist in the tropical regions. There are not set times for planting, and the suitability of growing an individual plant will depend on local climatic conditions.

Subtropical regions of the southern hemisphere (Australasia, South America, southern Africa)
The seasons are reversed in these regions. Spring is approximately from September to November, summer from December to February, autumn from March to May, and winter from June to August.

INDEX

Note: page numbers in **bold type** refer to illustrations